CAN'T YOU SMELL THE SMOKE?

A CHRISTIAN WOMAN'S JOURNEY DEALING WITH A NARCISSIST HUSBAND

SYDNEY KOH

WINGED PUBLICATIONS

Represented by AuthorizeMe Literary Firm,
Sharon Norris Elliott, Agent
PO BOX 1816, South Gate, CA 90280
www.AuthorizeMe.net
AuthorizeMeNow@gmail.com

Content Disclaimer: This book deals with certain sensitive issues that may trigger strong emotions in some people. While the author has endeavored to address these sensitive matters in a compassionate and respectful manner, the issues covered may trouble some readers.
Discretion is advised.

ISBN: 978-1-956654-89-9

To Mom and Dad...for encouraging me in countless ways.

To my boys, R/G/I...for being the answer to many of my whys in life.

To DG...for walking along this journey with me.

To all the silent victims of narcissistic abuse...I hope my story will bring you hope and remind you that God is there with you in your pain. You are not alone in this.

CONTENTS

A Free Gift for Our Readers

Did you just discover the difficult relationship in your life is with a narcissist?

I polled thousands of survivors and asked one question: What were the most impactful first steps you took in your narcissistic abuse recovery? This is what they told me.

Download your free guide below.

Your 7 Step Journey to Narcissistic Abuse Recovery

Includes:
- The key 7 strategies to kick start your healing
- The critical first step that has had the most impact for survivors
- How to create the ideal support system for your journey

- Bonus #1: Escape Plan Checklist
- Bonus #2: Anxiety Fighting Foods List
- Bonus #3: ebook *Self-Care Strategies for 24/7 Moms*

www.TrilliumSage.com

FOREWORD

~

My story is similar to Sydney Koh's in several ways: both of us were genuine Christians and highly educated, married highly educated Christian men who were clinically diagnosed with bipolar depression, our spouses stopped taking medication causing the marriage to deteriorate, we believed divorce was a grave sin and so resisted it, and when we eventually pursued divorced, we were guilt-stricken...

Sadly, our stories are not unique; there are countless Christian women who share these similarities. Many of them endure abusive marriages because they, too, are unaware of narcissistic abuse. All they have been taught is that God hates divorce; rarely do they hear that God hates abuse! I am so thankful that in His wonderful way, God used various people to help Sydney and me escape our abusive marriages.

I was a 25-year-old graduate student when I met the man of my dreams–a 32-year-old professor–at a renowned university. He and I dated for a year. Convinced that God was leading us to marry, we got engaged, and shortly thereafter exchanged wedding vows in a huge (yet beautiful) ceremony that was officiated by two ministers: the pastor of my local church and the pastor of his local church. I remember the joy and awe I felt deep in my soul as I listened to the pastors utter these solemn words to us: "Dearly beloved, we are gathered here in the sight of God, and in the presence of these witnesses, to join together this man and this woman in holy matrimony.... Marriage should not be entered into unadvisedly, but reverently, discreetly, and in the fear of God. Into this holy estate these two persons come now to be joined." After these words we exchanged our vows, swearing to remain faithful "...for better or for worse; for richer or for poorer; in sickness and in health ...till death do us part..." After our vows the minister sealed our fate by announcing, "What God has joined together let no man put asunder." With these grave words, I wiped away tears of joy, knowing that nothing except death would ever separate my beloved husband and me! What I received from my husband was not aligned with the vows we made.

Sadly, the marriage was horrible from the start. My husband and I had endless disagreements about anything and everything. What made the disagreements worse was how he attributed malice to everything I did and said. And whenever I would explain myself to help him understand my motive, he would call me argumentative. But I was determined that he understand that I loved him and had no ill motives, so I kept on explaining myself. Sometimes he said he understood, and I was happy we had solved the disagreement. But a few days later he would bring up the issue that we had just solved as though we had never discussed it. With time, he not only brought up issues that we had solved, but he started mixing up facts–confusing when and how certain events happened. We argued about that too... eventually I learned to hold my tongue because he loved using my words against me. He also loved going through my personal belongings searching for ammunition to use against me. One day, he read my private journal, then accused me of being a hypocrite, stating with a sneer, "Look how prideful and arrogant you are! You've admitted it right here by asking God to help you become humble!" I was furious he had read my journal, misunderstood what I wrote, and had the audacity to confront me rather than apologize for his actions. Instead of admitting he was wrong, he used my anger as evidence of my arrogance. When I defended myself, he interpreted it as evidence of defiant spirit. There was no winning–I was doomed if I defended myself; I was doomed if I didn't! The best I could do was walk on eggshells, doing my best to avoid upsetting him with either my words or my silence.

Barely two years after our wedding, my husband and I were forced into counseling. He had slapped me and threatened to break my jaw if I did not leave the house immediately. During the counseling session, the counselor (a Christian psychiatrist) informed us that the violence had occurred because my husband had stopped taking his antidepressants. He then advised us to separate until my husband's mental condition was stabilized. I stared at him in disbelief and replied, "I swore to love my husband in sickness and in health. I cannot leave him now that he is sick." The psychiatrist told me that if I did not leave, there was danger of my husband killing me in another fit of psychotic rage. "My husband is a Christian, and he could never kill me. Besides, God says that no weapon formed against me shall prosper!" I replied with deep conviction. I now shudder at my naïve confidence.

To understand where I was coming from, it is important to point out that, just like Sydney, I grew up in a Christian family where I was taught that God hates divorce. For this reason, I was determined to remain in that marriage–only death would separate us!

Mercifully, while I was still arguing with the psychiatrist, my husband agreed to the separation. He also asked that we pray daily, asking God to heal him quickly so that we could get back together as soon as possible. Unfortunately, instead of getting better during our separation, he became worse. He started accusing me of trying to leave him for another man, accusing my pastor of not doing enough to keep me in check, writing long letters to friends telling them how terrible I was... Sadly, many friends believed him because on the outside, he was a quiet and very godly young man. Long story short, the worse he treated me during those months we were separated, the more my eyes opened to his cruelty. Eventually I left the country for further studies, and while away, I battled my conscience, overcame my upbringing, and started the divorce proceedings.

As a result of our past, Sydney and I work closely in a private group that helps Christian victims of narcissistic abuse. I thank God for her because I have seen the beautiful way in which she uses her life experience to give invaluable advice to victims. In addition to the valuable advice, I have witnessed Sydney extend a heart of compassion as she shares her story with them.

It is my sincere prayer that everyone who reads Sydney's story will recognize narcissistic abuse for what it is and do whatever they can to protect themselves (and their children) from further abuse–without being guilt-stricken.

Dr. Njeri Bere
Professor of Sociology, Lincoln Christian University
(Retired)
Indigenous Missionary working with the Maasai in Kenya

1

UNKNOWN CALLER

"Unknown Caller."

The flashing itself was enough to startle me, and the ominous "unknown" made it even worse.

The red numbers on the clock read 10:33pm. So, my speculation began. The two "unknown callers" I knew were my best friend, Danielle, and my mom. *Hmm...Danielle knows me well enough to know that I don't like talking on the phone, much less talking when I could be sleeping. She would've warned me with a text before calling. Is it Mom? Is something wrong with Mom?*

I picked up, preparing myself for the worst. "Hello?"

A low, unfamiliar male voice greeted me. *OK, definitely not my mom.*

"Mrs. Silver? This is Officer Baker with the Orange County Sheriff's Department. Is Ben Silver your husband?"

"Yes, what's going on?" This call was beginning to worry me.

"I'm afraid I have some bad news to share. Mr. Silver shot himself."

"What?! Well, is he okay?" My immediate thought was that the shooting was some kind of accident, but then the past three days leading up to this moment flashed through my mind.

"I'm sorry for your loss." Officer Baker used the phrase that only meant one thing. It finally hit me. Ben was dead.

My legs felt weak. As I collapsed on the couch, the officer droned on about how Crystal, Ben's sister, had found him. After multiple unsuccessful attempts to contact him, she had gone to his apartment, fearing the worst. When he didn't answer the door, she used her key to enter and discovered him on the bathroom floor. As she called 911, she still held out hope, but the paramedics confirmed that he was gone.

My mind immediately went in a million different directions, darting from the shocking information that Officer Baker was relaying to me, to my three young sons living without a father, to the steps I needed to take next. My hands started to feel tingly, and then the more intense pins and needles took over. *Oh, Officer Baker is still talking to me.* My brain allowed me to collect myself quickly enough to jot down some information–phone numbers, the case number, the police report, the coroner. Everything moved in a strange accelerated slow motion. It all felt like a dream. Or a nightmare.

Officer Baker mentioned that the boys' schools would be contacted so that they were aware of the situation, and I interrupted him. "Gosh, how do I even tell the kids?" He suggested telling my eldest, Ryan, alone first, and then together we would break the news to the younger boys, Greg and Isaac.

The call seemed to end as quickly as it started. Truly stunned at the news, I couldn't believe the amount of grief that washed over me for the man who had abused me for the last eight years. *How can I possibly be this distraught?*

Ryan came downstairs, curious about the late-night phone call. There was not enough time to process it, let alone address Ryan's concern. He asked what was going on. I explained that I just got off the phone with a police officer.

For a sixth-grader, Ryan probably has more street smarts and awareness than most kids his age. "Was it about Papa?" he asked.

Not having much time to consider the best way to deliver the news, I slowly responded. "Yes."

Without hesitation, Ryan then asked point blank, "Was Papa in a drunk driving accident?" I had instructed Ryan to never get into the car if Ben had been drinking, so this question was in line with what he had been taught.

I made a split-second decision to just answer as truthfully and as simply as I could. "No, he wasn't in a drunk driving accident..." I had to pause to say the next thing just right, "...but he is in Heaven now."

Ryan's eyes widened. "No!" he cried in a raised voice. He wept inconsolably and muttered, "I just wish I had more time with him." This was the same kid who had grudgingly asked me three days prior, "Why do I have to keep going to Papa's?" It appears that I wasn't alone in my struggle with mixed emotions.

Ryan waited a short moment before his next question. "Did he use his gun?"

I only nodded.

Ryan had never cried the way he did that night. It was a raw emotion that only comes in such a devastating circumstance. As I held Ryan's quivering body, every few moments he paused to tell me something insightful or to ask a line of questions that obviously came from thoughts he had privately pondered for quite a while:

"You don't have to pay your lawyer anymore."

"Are we going to have enough money?"

"We have to tell the brothers."

"Do we have to sell the house?"

I assured Ryan, "I don't have all the answers, but I'll figure it out. We're a strong family, we have many people who care about us, and we're going to get through this. Most importantly, God will walk with us through this as He has done in previous years with other difficult situations."

Was this actually God's protection for us?

It was never supposed to be like this. Ben's sudden passing confused me. Our divorce had been almost finalized, but despite our separation, I wanted Ben to be the father I had prayed he would be to our boys. Couldn't God turn everything around? Of course, He could, because He's God. But now that possibility was forever taken off the table.

I tried to make sense of the news, wondering where God was in this crazy mess. He had played a prominent role in my life, especially in recent years. Falling back on all that God had done for us, all I could do was continue to trust in His faithfulness. With God as our Rock, I once again found myself relying on Him and took comfort in that. *Listen, God, I have no idea what to think right now. Just please be near us.*

Ryan suddenly stopped crying, turned to me with his big wet eyes, and asked one final question for the night.

"Can we get a dog?"

∾

God Sightings

When facing traumatic life events--abuse, divorce, the unexpected death of a loved one--God may seem distant, but He's actually closer than ever. It just may be that it's harder to recognize Him in the crowd of troubles. Chapter 29 of this book will serve as a point of reflection where we will stop, scan over the current circumstances, and I will point out how I found God still there, still close, still caring. Believe it or not, very much still in charge of everything.

Journal Prompts

Journaling is a highly effective way of taking a moment to reflect on life's challenges. Because this is a personal expression of one's emotions, often containing sensitive information, it is advised that you take care to protect your privacy as you write out your thoughts and feelings. If you are living with an abusive spouse, keeping your journal with a trusted friend rather than at home may be something to consider. Journal prompts for each chapter, along with Scripture and prayer starters, are also found in Chapter 29.

HAPPIER TIMES

"Hey, wanna be lab partners?"

Quickly scanning the lab, I was disappointed to find that I had no other viable options besides Ben. I subtly rolled my eyes and sighed a reluctant "Sure." Dang it, he was my new lab partner.

And this wasn't any ordinary university chemistry lab. It was an upper-level inorganic chemistry lab that met once a week. For nine hours each week. For ten weeks. *Ugh, what did I just get myself into?*

It wasn't that Ben wasn't a nice guy at the time. I just found him incredibly annoying. In fact, I used to go to our shared class lectures intentionally late so I could see where he sat and sit a healthy distance away from him. All this trouble was just so I wouldn't have to say 'hi.' We had met through a mutual friend two years prior in 1993, at a study session, and to me, he was just kind of nerdy. Every interaction I had with him had resulted in a conversation about professors and classes. How dreadfully boring!

Well, those ten weeks changed everything. Ben would

jokingly recall later that he "grew on me...like a fungus." Maybe it was the chemical fumes in the lab, but I actually started to see past the nerdy facade. He was charming, highly intelligent, and had a clever sense of humor. When our lab ended after those ten weeks, Ben and I started dating.

It was our senior year in college, and we soon graduated. Most of my friends were headed to graduate school or launching directly into their careers, but neither option was attractive to me. After graduation, I pictured myself moving back to my birth country, Singapore, to explore Asia and find a job for a few years. Now, with Ben in my life, it would be difficult to be apart, but we both agreed that I would go ahead and move to Singapore. I found a job at a hospital lab there while Ben started his graduate program in chemical physics in Irvine, California.

Long distance relationships are never easy. They were even more difficult before the internet was a part of daily life. As international calls were expensive, we rarely communicated by phone. In 1995, the internet was just in its beginning stages, but being as tech savvy as he was, Ben introduced me to email, and we communicated by a very rudimentary version of chat if we happened to be online at the same time. The sixteen-hour time difference was a huge challenge, too. We caught up with each other every day via email until one day when I didn't hear from him. I figured he was busy with his graduate program. I knew his lab experiments ran long, so I interpreted this silence as either his busyness with school or his necessity for rest between experiments. But then one day stretched into two. Something was definitely off, and I started to worry.

Ben eventually got back in touch and told me about the difficulties he was facing. Between the stress of school and life in general, he found himself awake all hours of the night and depressed. His graduate program kept him working for hours on end. Ben saw a doctor, and upon a detailed evaluation of his mental health history through the years, the doctor diagnosed him with bipolar depression.

Ben was put on medication and was hopeful that it would stabilize his mood. After a few weeks, he told me that the medication seemed to be working, he was feeling much better, and he now had a more positive outlook on life.

During the time we were apart, I went back to California once and Ben visited me in Singapore once. We decided that if we were serious about our relationship, we really should be living in the same time zone. So, after being apart for 20 months, I moved back to Southern California.

Two years after my return, we celebrated our nuptials in Palos Verdes, California, with two hundred of our closest friends and family. Ben started his career at a well-known automotive company, and I worked in the biotechnology sector. We bought our first home in Orange County, California, and enjoyed the freedom and fun that came with being a DINKs (dual-income, no kids) household. Since I traveled frequently for business, we used my miles and points to vacation extensively. That business travel, though, meant that for a while, I was away for most of the week, and we really only got to spend time together on the weekends.

Looking back now, those peaceful times may have been mostly due to my absence. In hindsight, I should have recognized the first of many red flags to come. One weekend, Ben and I returned from an errand, and I parked the car in the driveway. He casually commented that the car didn't seem straight, so I backed up, straightened out, and re-parked it. Thinking that was it, I turned off the engine and unbuckled my seatbelt. Again, Ben said that the car wasn't straight. I remember wondering whether he was joking, and when I realized from the deadpan look on his face that he wasn't, I simply told him that the car *was* straight and if he didn't think it was, he could re-park it himself. I walked into the house thinking, *That was odd,* but just brushed it off to Ben's perfectionism. Little did I know that this perfectionism wasn't something to brush off.

After four years of marriage, the idea of starting a family became more of a reality. I always looked forward to having kids, having grown up as the eldest of three in my own family. We welcomed our first son, Ryan, in 2004. Soon after Ryan's arrival, Ben and I decided to make whatever necessary sacrifices it would take to enable me to stay home to raise our family. As we were still in the early years of our careers, if I stopped working, our household income would be reduced by half. In order to live comfortably under these conditions, we realized we might have to move to a different state to make the finances work.

Ben began his job search and networked with some of his out-of-state contacts. We brainstormed a few cities and states that would make sense to us: somewhere on the West Coast, easy access to Asian markets, and opportunity in Ben's field of business. A few months after he began his search, a well-known Seattle technology company reached out to him with an opportunity. It wasn't even a company that Ben had considered! As he was interviewing with this company, another reputable technology company, also based in the Seattle area, contacted Ben with a position they were hoping he could fill. Seeing that both of these companies were in the Seattle area, we were excited as we felt God's hand nudging us to Washington. Ben interviewed with both companies and accepted one of the positions.

Shortly before Ryan's first birthday, we found ourselves and all our possessions making the trek from Southern California to our new home in the Pacific Northwest. We were excited at the prospect of our new reality that I would be able to stay home with Ryan full-time. We loved our new environment and would often comment to each other how unbelievable it was that we were able to live in such a beautiful part of the country. I never tired of the abundance of green trees on the hillsides and the wispy clouds between them. One thing that didn't occur to us until we moved was just how much we would miss our closest friends and family.

A few months after Ben started his job, he came home with a dark cloud over him. We all have bad days, so I didn't think too much of it. Then, a few days later, the same thing happened. A pattern began to develop, and he was coming home upset more often than not. I could tell he was stressed, and he confessed that he was starting to worry his new job wasn't the right fit for him.

Soon after, things quickly unraveled, and Ben broke down and told me just how stressed he was. His new work environment was terribly unprofessional, and he was held responsible for issues that he inherited when he filled the vacated role. He was hysterical as he painted an image for me of his work life. I had never seen him this vulnerable before, and I was frightened that he was spiraling out of control. My parents happened to be in town, and they watched Ryan while I drove Ben to the nearest emergency room.

We didn't exchange many words on the drive as I tried to figure out how best to help Ben. I finally broke the silence. "You know, your job isn't your whole life. If it's not a good fit, let's get you out of there. No job is worth your mental health." Ben hesitantly agreed. We saw a doctor, who prescribed anti-anxiety medication for Ben's panic attacks.

Ben submitted his resignation later that same week. We put ourselves on a shoestring budget to be most financially efficient, not knowing just how long it would be until Ben found his next job. For the next five months, we lived off our savings. Each passing day brought increasing discomfort because we had no idea when Ben would get his next job. At what point do we stop bleeding our savings? All the while, we prayed that God would continue to provide for us. In that season of drought and unknowns, we realized just how much we truly missed our loved ones back in California.

This time of uncertainty caused Ben to become more irritable. I understood that this was expected, given our situation. Little annoyances became big blow-ups. Issues that Ben would typically allow to slide were now major roadblocks. On one occasion, our neighbor did something minor to annoy Ben, and he took it upon himself to confront the neighbor about the imposition. It was embarrassing to watch Ben fixate on trivial matters and strain relationships unnecessarily.

As Ben continued his search and networked with old contacts, he happened to speak with his former manager. His manager told Ben that he'd always have a job waiting for him if he wanted to move back to California. And as if that wasn't good enough news, his manager offered him a pay raise! With Ben's new salary, we realized that we could make it on his income alone in Southern California. And as an added bonus, we would be back home with the friends and family we treasured. It took a six-month absence and 1200 miles for us to learn the hard way the real importance of the people we held most dear.

We moved back to California, settled into our new home, and reconnected with everyone that we missed. Ben was happy to be working at his old company in his new role, and I continued enjoying the privilege of being a stay-at-home mom to Ryan.

Soon, in 2006, our family grew again. Ben had always wanted a daughter. We shared this comment with the labor and delivery nurse, and when the doctor announced Greg's arrival–a boy–she turned to us and said, "OK, see you in two years!" Two years and a day later, we walked into the labor and delivery suite and asked if that same nurse was working the shift. She was, and remembering our conversation, she was eager to find out what would happen in the delivery room this time. That December evening in 2008, we celebrated the arrival of baby Isaac. Another boy! Having another rambunctious, energy-zapping son frightened both of us, and we decided that our family was complete with our three sweet boys. Ben's wishes for a daughter were dashed.

Our young family kept us busy, and in those early years, our day-to-day life was not unlike many other young families: diapers, cleaning up spills, Tooth Fairy visits, ice cream runs, laundry, and sporting events. Weekends were spent on soccer fields, at the kung fu studio, at home entertaining friends, attending church events, and in the kitchen in our quest to make the perfect breakfast burrito.

From the outside, we pretty much had the perfect little family. We lived in a beautiful home with our three boys. Ben continued to excel in his career and received recognition as a key player in the various companies for which he worked.

Still, the saying is true: all that glitters is not gold. Little annoyances kept popping up, and it was a never-ending game of Whack-a-Mole. As I juggled life with the three boys, I started to realize that I wasn't simply a stay-at-home mom—I was almost living as a single mom while married. I noticed that Ben was not remotely involved with the boys' basic needs and daily care. One evening as I was nursing Isaac, Ben walked into the room and flatly informed me that Greg needed a diaper change. I told him that I'd appreciate it if he could change him, since I was occupied, and Isaac had feeding issues. To my surprise, Ben simply said, "That's okay, Greg can wait till you're done."

From that moment on, I began observing more situations in which Ben had the opportunity to lend a hand but chose to fulfill his needs over his sons' needs. Little things like getting food for himself while I struggled to prepare food for the boys became increasingly more noticeable. I'm not one to compare, but I did take note that other fathers were much more involved than Ben with the raising of their children. *Well, maybe it's because Ben was the youngest in his family growing up or because he's never had a stable father figure in his life? Maybe he's never had it modeled to him before?* I continued making excuses to justify Ben's hands-off approach.

On one particularly busy day, I brought this up to Ben, and his response was simply that he provides for our family financially, and he assumed I would take care of any and all of the "kid stuff." I explained that while I am happy to care for our kids, and I definitely don't expect him to do as much as I do, I would appreciate him lending a hand. The littlest gesture would make a tremendous difference. He agreed to help, but this turned out to be an empty promise.

As I continued to care for the boys, others began noticing

Ben's lack of involvement as well. Those closest to me would ask, "Why doesn't Ben help you more?" I always found a way to make a convenient excuse for him. The reality was that I didn't want to confront him and figured that since I had the strength and energy, I could manage just fine. The few times I did bring it up to him, I was met with snappy words and harsh tones. Ben's common go-to was, "Do you know how much I already do for our family?" It was easier for me to handle things on my own than involve him and the inevitable argument.

Ben seemed to occupy his time at home on a very predictable schedule. On weekdays, he would come home from work, make himself an adult beverage, eat dinner, play with the boys for a little bit, and go to bed. On weekends, Saturdays were all about sports, and Sundays were reserved for church and his chores. His Sunday chores took a great deal of time as Ben was meticulous about things like backing up his computer and organizing files. The more time he spent on his chores, the more he withdrew from the kids. When I noticed this, I implemented a new Sunday afternoon plan. Instead of rushing home after church, we would be intentional about spending time together as a family. Whether it be a picnic lunch at the park, a short hike on a local trail, or a quick trip to the beach, the important thing was that we were to spend time as a family–and hopefully, Ben would be able to engage more with the boys.

Our new plan worked for a couple of months, but as time went on, Ben would start asking earlier and earlier when we could go home because he had to attend to his Sunday chores. I tried to persuade him that while I recognize his chores are important to him, it's far more important to be more involved with his sons and our family. I began to feel as if Ben was my fourth son, another child for me to train.

It was about this time that I started to feel rather overwhelmed with my role in the family. Why was Ben increasingly only caring for himself? Did he not see with his own two eyes that I was running around crazily caring for the boys? Again, I convinced myself that I was strong enough to do this on my own. I made a commitment to raising my boys to the best of my ability and creating memories of the best childhood ever for them. If Ben wanted to be a part of it, he would have to do so on his own terms. I took the boys camping with friends, to the petting zoo, on beach trips, to the pumpkin patch, anywhere I knew the boys would enjoy. Ben found a way to excuse himself from most of these activities.

In addition to his lack of engagement with the boys, Ben's attitude at home started to change. His obsession with cleanliness ramped up to a menacing level, and he would constantly be on the boys for dropping crumbs as they ate. When we had friends over, he had no qualms about imposing this on our friends' children as well, which made for many uncomfortable situations. Dropped crumbs, spilled juice, and minor messes always brought on a far more serious reaction than necessary when Ben was in the room. When the boys and I heard the garage door open, we knew that we now had to watch every little step lest we upset Ben.

One event made me question if Ben was still the same man I married. I had been searching for an old high school friend with whom I had lost touch. Since I had recently opened a social media account, I hoped to reconnect with people, but none as much as this particular friend. I was excited to see her name pop up when I searched for her, but a split second later, I was absolutely devastated when I discovered that her name led to a memorial page about her. It turns out she had been a victim of a hit and run on New Year's Eve a few years prior. I crumbled as my thrilling search came to such a sudden and mournful end. When I shared this with Ben, instead of receiving some sort of consolation or comfort from him, he simply said, "Well, you haven't seen her in decades anyway." His lack of empathy was startling, and I was quite shocked and genuinely disgusted. Something was going on with Ben, and I wasn't sure what it was or if I was just imagining things. *God, seriously, what is this?!*

I began to take mental notes of these occasions. I'm not sure what happened to the kind man I knew and loved. He seemed to be fading away slowly each passing day. As this new normal continued, my parents grew increasingly concerned that I would burn out as I cared for our family on my own. They had no idea of the other stressful home situations I faced with Ben's personality quirks, which changed each day. Since my younger sister, Merissa, was getting married overseas and summer was fast approaching, my mother suggested that I take an extended vacation to rest in Singapore–without Ben. It was a convenient excuse for some much-needed distance, and surprisingly, Ben agreed that the boys would enjoy being in Singapore for more than the usual two-week vacations we had taken in the past. We spent the best six weeks of our lives that summer in Singapore. Carefree. Not on eggshells. Doing and saying what we honestly wanted to do and say without fear of reprimand. My parents commented that I seemed less stressed and better rested. This was an obvious and undeniable truth. I was, and I could tell that my boys were as well. This time and distance away from Ben proved beneficial for each of us.

When our dream vacation came to an end, we returned home to California. I was nervous to see Ben again after such a long time, and I didn't know what to expect as we walked into the terminal. My anxiety about our reunion melted away quickly when he greeted us at the airport with a big smile and tight hugs. Later, while the boys played, he shared that he realized our extended time in Singapore was not simply a vacation, but a necessary break from him and the stressful home environment he had created. He vowed to make serious changes so that our home would be more peaceful. It was exactly what I had hoped our trip would accomplish. The question now was whether or not Ben would be able to keep up his end of the bargain.

THE SIMMER BEGINS

For two full weeks after our return from Singapore, I was thrilled to have the old Ben back in my life. He was caring, loving, respectful, and helpful. He made an intentional effort with his words and actions. Once during those two weeks, he made a cutting remark but quickly recoiled and apologized. I could tell he was really trying, and I praised God for this drastic change. For the first time in many years, the boys had fun playing with Ben, and I could see that they enjoyed their relationship with him. As they ran around the house chasing each other with Nerf guns and shouting with excitement, I hoped I'd continue to see what I'd wanted for our family for so long.

Unfortunately, those two weeks were all we had. Suddenly, Ben reverted to his abusive ways. I noticed he was drinking more than before. And as he continued to climb in his career, he grew more confident–to the point of being prideful. I once commented to Ben that God has blessed him with some pretty incredible work opportunities. Ben responded, "Well, I work really hard." I'm not denying that

Ben worked hard, but instead of appreciating God's blessings and timely circumstances, Ben attributed his success solely to his own merit. I grew concerned that his lack of humility would catch up to him and be his downfall as I recalled Proverbs 16:18: "Pride goes before destruction, and a haughty spirit before a fall."

Later that year, Ben encountered a painful medical condition that forced him to make a major lifestyle change. He was ordered to dramatically change his diet. Over the course of a year, with his new diet in place, he lost over sixty pounds. Ben grew even more confident now that he was no longer overweight. He continued to find success in his career, especially after back-to-back promotions. With his newfound confidence and achievements, he claimed that he was misdiagnosed with bipolar depression and took himself off the medications that he started in graduate school. I told him that he can't just do that. It was a decision that needed to be made with the approval and guidance of his psychiatrist. Ben disagreed and made the executive decision to go off his medications. This was to be the beginning of the end.

I found myself in more frequent and more contentious situations with Ben. Any spoken word to him had to be thoughtfully considered in order to decrease the odds of his verbal wrath. One day I came home to find a new tissue box cover in our master bathroom. It really was not to my liking. I contemplated how I was to state my dislike without causing Ben to overreact. I finally decided that I wouldn't say anything unless he asked. He came home later that day and, sure enough, asked what I thought about the new tissue box cover. I took a deep breath as I prepared to tell him the honest truth that I didn't like it.

"To be perfectly honest," I said, "it's not one I would have chosen."

Thinking that was the most subtle way of relaying my opinion, I hoped for a calm response, but I was sorely disappointed. Ben launched into a tirade: "Well, next time YOU buy it then!"

I even told him that I knew he would overreact to my disagreeing with this choice and spent way more time than anyone should on how to carefully share an honest opinion. He yelled, "And that's the best you came up with?!" as he stormed out of the room.

It didn't matter whether I was at fault–I would still be on the losing end. As Ben continued as the breadwinner for the family, my main contribution was staying within my budget for various things like groceries, clothing, and household items. One day when Ben was reviewing our finances, he approached me and informed me that I went $300 over on groceries. I was shocked because I hadn't changed my buying habits that month. I asked to see the numbers and realized that the $300 difference was Ben's shopping spree at the liquor store. When I pointed this out to him, instead of apologizing for automatically blaming me, he calmly said that he wouldn't have to self-medicate his depression with alcohol if it weren't for me.

Unfortunately, my parents had to witness Ben's behavior firsthand. One fall Saturday, my parents came to visit and watch the younger boys while we took Ryan to a kung fu tournament an hour away in Los Angeles. Knowing that we were pressed for time, I told Ben that I would make him oatmeal and it would be ready in 15 minutes. Ben finally came down 15 minutes later than planned, took one look at his breakfast, and asked if I could reheat it. As I was busy getting Ryan's kung fu gear together, I told him that I wouldn't be able to, but he could warm it up in the microwave if he would like. He was not satisfied with that answer and asked if I could make him fresh oatmeal on the stove. I was obviously annoyed at this point, but when he shouted, "Can you look at me when I'm talking to you?" from across the room, I felt my face redden with embarrassment that my parents had to see this themselves. Judging from the look on their faces, I knew they were becoming aware of my reality. Thankfully, Ben's rage went no further than his grumpiness that morning, and we left without him having any breakfast.

A few weeks later after that incident, my parents came to visit. My mom took me aside and with a concerned look on her face asked me if Ben had ever hit me. I was shocked that she would even ask such a question and quickly answered, "No!" Then, recalling what she had witnessed with her very own eyes several weeks ago, I realized that the question wasn't so out of line. If he was treating me the way my parents saw firsthand, they must wonder how he treated me when they weren't around.

This was getting out of control, and up to this point, I was dealing with Ben and these situations on my own. I was also having a lot of bold conversations with God. I desperately wanted to protect Ben, and I didn't share these events with even my closest friends. I knew something was going on but was not sure what it was. All I knew was that I didn't want others finding out about these tumultuous moments. I was determined to find out what was going on, and I was willing to fix Ben on my own to save him from embarrassment.

Acknowledging he was now at a more senior level at

work with far more responsibilities, I assumed the work stress was the major contributor to his behavior. I tried to be understanding, but Ben found fault in, and criticized, everything I did. I realized that for my own sanity, I could no longer keep this to myself. I decided that I would share with Danielle, my best friend, to get her take on my situation.

THE PENNY DROPS

"It's bad."

I didn't know how else to start. I looked around the sunny restaurant patio where Danielle and I sat. People were laughing, children were running around, and the sound of birds chirping engulfed us. Looking around, I curiously wondered, *How can they possibly not sense the profound pain I feel?* The carefree energy of our surroundings was a stark contrast to the dark and lonely hell I was privately living. I don't remember many details of how or what I shared with Danielle that day. I do remember later Danielle recalling that she felt the immense desperation in my situation as I finally confessed the truth about my home life. Trapped. Hopeless. Frustrated. I had so many strong emotions but no idea what to do about them.

After two long years of a difficult marriage, I finally shared the truth with Danielle, and she admitted that she wasn't all that surprised. She and her husband, Frank, always wondered how I put up with Ben. As one of our closest friends, for better or for worse, she'd seen our true colors.

Between Ben and me, he was far more rigid, and I was more flexible. It was just easier for me to adjust to situations, so I did. However, in doing so through the years, I had lost myself.

This, of course, came as no surprise to Danielle. She has known me since I was ten years old when my mom hired her to drive my siblings and me to our after-school activities. Just a short five years my senior, she is someone I deeply respect for her wisdom and insight. Through our decades-friendship, she has helped me through various life stages. Danielle has always played the role as my most ardent protector, ever-willing wine-tasting partner, tireless prayer warrior, creative problem solver, and reliable source of encouragement. I count her as one of God's blessings in my life. She is, quite simply, the Jonathan to my David.

Knowing how much pain I was in, Danielle naturally wanted to immediately remedy the situation. As a first step, she encouraged me to seek God as these circumstances were much larger than either of us knew how to handle. She assured me that she would be praying over Ben and me as I tried to figure things out.

Leaving our lunch, I felt somewhat lighter now that I had verbalized the pain that was privately consuming me. I decided that it might be beneficial to seek counsel from other women I trusted. In the days and weeks following, I prayed and asked God to show me the people who might be able to help me push through this difficult phase in my marriage. Of course, God is God–He didn't disappoint.

God put it in my heart to seek out believers I already held in high regard. I first met with my old Bible study leaders, Jill and Delia. We discussed Ben's mental health, and they shared their experiences in handling similar mental health issues within their own families. They understood me in my confusion, and I was able to pose one of the most pressing questions that kept my mind spinning. *How can I both respectfully stand up for myself and honor my husband as he kills my spirit with his words?* Just like Danielle, they suggested seeking God through this and to listen earnestly for His voice, wisdom, and guidance. Jill and Delia encouraged me that no matter what Ben doled out, I needed to listen to what God would expect me to do even in the most challenging of circumstances. Jill seared one particular concept into my brain when she said, "Sydney, remember that the mountaintop is glorious, but the valley is lush and where the flowers grow." I was impacted by her reminder that the valley *is* lush, and I would later hear her voice utter those very words in my head on my toughest days.

Next, I sought out mentors within my church. I met with three women in our congregation who I viewed as godly, wise women. The kind of women who make living as a Proverbs 31 woman look like a walk in the park. Time spent with these friends always brought comfort. They prayed over me, my marriage, my sons, and, most of all, Ben. They knew him as the kind and charming persona he portrayed in public and were shocked to hear what went on behind the closed doors of our home. The stories I shared were incongruent with the man they greeted each week at our Sunday church service.

One of the women advised me to reach out to Belle, a friend of hers. She didn't give me more information than letting me know that I might gain some support from her. I reached out to Belle, and when we met up for brunch, I explained my situation. She shared her story and how she escaped a toxic relationship by leaving her husband to live in a women's shelter with her young children. Her story was particularly encouraging to me because her husband was able to get the necessary help, and they eventually reconciled and enjoyed a newfound love in their marriage. Despite the torture and madness I was going through with Ben, I ultimately wanted the same: for us to get over this troubling time in our marriage. Belle gave me a renewed hope to fight for my marriage and reminded me that with God, the impossible *is* possible.

With every interaction I had, I walked away with a new idea, a new direction, or a new strategy from the encouragement of my Christian community. Many days I felt stagnant, but when I was pushed to take even the tiniest baby steps, knowing I was making progress in the right direction greatly encouraged me. The assurance that I had an army of prayer warriors backing me up further strengthened me. I realized that as lonely as I felt in my fight for my marriage, I was never truly alone in this battle. God put people in my path to serve as His messengers, and I came to realize this truth even more as time progressed.

AS YOU WISH

Comforted by the support I had already received from the few friends I shared my story with, I was energized and motivated to take a new approach with Ben. I wanted so desperately to make him happy in our home but had no idea what that might entail. I decided I would employ the strategy of simply killing him with kindness.

For one month straight, I did everything I could do to make Ben happy. Whether it was cooking his favorite meals, making sure the house was impeccably neat, or monitoring the kids' behavior, I gave it my all. To tell you the truth, at this point in time, *I* would have loved being married to me! When the month was over, I saw that Ben still found fault with me, and at this very moment, I realized I would never be enough for him. If my best would never be good enough for him, why should I bother trying? But even more importantly, what did this mean for our future as husband and wife?

I cried out to God because He was the one constant in the ever-changing landscape of my quickly deteriorating home life. Even then, Ben attacked me. Because the kids were so young, I rarely had the opportunity to go out with friends, much less have any sort of social life outside of the kids and Ben. The one thing that I did for myself was a weekly Bible study at a local church. I immensely enjoyed this break once a week when I was able to carve out some time just for me. No kids, guaranteed hot coffee, diving into the Word–what's not to love? This was a solid Bible-teaching church, and each week when I dropped off the boys in the children's program to meet with my group, I knew I was going to leave church that day a little bit lighter, more motivated, and ready to continue working on my marriage. As I prepared for my Bible study one night, Ben pulled up a chair next to me and plainly stated, "I think you're too religious. They're brainwashing you." I've never been a fan of the word "religious" because it implies rigidity and legalism, and it doesn't capture the true relationship that I have with God and my faith. Ironically, little did Ben know that on many occasions, these Bible study mornings gave me just enough fuel to even *desire* my marriage.

Ben insisted I discontinue attending the Bible study. I was exasperated that he had now taken away the one weekly event that meant so much to me. I discussed this new development with my Bible study leaders, and although they were sad to see me leave the group, they understood the uncomfortable situation I was in. They did encourage me to continue seeking God in ways that wouldn't disrupt my marriage. The frustration from the inability to even spend time with God as I wished really started making me resent Ben.

I shared this latest predicament of discontinuing my weekly Bible study at the church with my close friend, Leah, and without hesitation, she blurted, "I'll do Bible study with you then!" I was thrilled by her enthusiasm and willingness to ensure I was still fed despite Ben's wishes. We came up with a plan to choose a book to work through together. I was open to any and all ideas. She suggested the Beth Moore study, *A Woman's Heart: God's Dwelling Place*. I didn't think much of the book until we dove into our weekly sessions. Once a week, Leah and I would take turns meeting at each other's homes over fresh coffee and overly indulgent buttery baked goods. This book was incredibly timely as it spoke of the Israelites and their journey with the tabernacle through the wilderness. I was definitely able to relate to being in the wilderness given the state of my marriage. Spending time in God's Word and remembering His truths and promises picked up right where my old Bible study left off. I was excited to have an alternative and grateful for a friend who was willing to keep me in the Word.

ENCOURAGEMENT FROM AFAR

I n the summer of 2013, just before school started, my parents invited our family to join them for a trip to Hawaii. Knowing how stressed I was in my marriage, they thoughtfully offered this time away to allow me to decompress. We excitedly told the boys that we were taking a family vacation with some of their favorite people in the world, their grandparents, to Maui. This would be the first time the boys visited Hawaii, and I knew, without a doubt, that they would absolutely love it. Spending seven days in board shorts and rash guards at the beach, chasing the island's green geckos, eating shave ice (not shaved ice) and spam musubi–how could they not? I had to temper my excitement knowing that Ben would be traveling with us as well–I had to be realistic about our upcoming vacation.

The balmy island breeze greeted us as soon as we stepped off the plane. We checked into the hotel and decided to ease into our vacation by lounging by the pool that first afternoon. We found a shady spot by the kids' pool and settled in.

As Ben moved an additional lounge chair to where we were sitting, he stubbed his toe. I could tell he was in pain, but it didn't seem like it was that bad an injury. I didn't realize that this injury would be his way of getting out of helping with the kids for the remainder of our trip.

The beginning of the trip was great, but with each day, Ben grew increasingly less helpful in every way. It was strange that even though we were on vacation as a family, it seemed more like I was on vacation with the boys and my parents, and Ben was just there with us. Every invitation of "Ben, can you..." was met with, "I can't because my toe hurts." I could tell that my parents were annoyed with Ben's convenient excuse to participate in any meaningful way.

As with any vacation, the trip seemed to end just as quickly as it began. We soon found ourselves back at the airport, ready to head home. Like any mom traveling with three kids under the age of nine, I was prepared to board as efficiently as possible. I asked Ben to help, and he offered to board with Ryan, now nine. I asked him to help with one of the younger boys instead, since Ryan was already pretty independent. Ben refused, and I was left with the two younger boys and our carry-on bags. Thankfully, my parents were there with extra hands to help.

We arrived home, and just before my parents hopped into their car for the drive back to their house, my mom quickly pulled me aside and said something that surprised me: "Syd, your marriage doesn't have to be a death sentence." I had tried to hide the misery of my marriage from my parents, but my mom is very intuitive and could see what was really going on. Her simple statement took a tremendous weight off my shoulders.

Back to reality with the boys back at school. Each morning, I silenced my alarm clock, took a deep breath, and prayed that today would be easier than the previous day. Unfortunately, the opposite was true: each passing day with Ben was becoming *harder.* The insults, the disparaging remarks, the criticism, and the rages were increasing not only in frequency, but also in intensity.

I dragged my body out of bed, got ready, and carried on with my morning duties: getting the kids ready for school, making breakfasts and lunches for the family, and sending the boys off to school and Ben off to work.

As soon as I heard the garage door slam down when Ben left for work, I breathed a sigh of relief knowing that for at least the next eight hours I would be able to be me. The me that was relaxed and a bit more carefree, with my head clear of any negativity brought on by Ben. I could enjoy some peace for this eight-hour block of time.

The days were filled with fun and laughter as I spent time with the kids after school. Catching up on what went on at school that day, goofing off, doing homework, eating snacks, playing around the house–we were all so at ease. Even the boys' fights among themselves were bearable.

However, around six o'clock in the evening, I could feel my body tense up knowing that within the hour, our garage door would roar open, and Ben would walk through the door. My dread was all-consuming. Because I knew the boys' naturally boisterous behavior stressed Ben out, I would often feed the boys dinner ahead of time and send them off to shower before he arrived home.

I hope Ben had a good day at work today. I would pray that each evening, hoping he would be a bit lighter. This was rarely the case, and regardless of how his day went, I knew that from the moment he entered the house, I would be walking on eggshells again until he went to bed or passed out from one too many drinks. I didn't even mind him passing out because it meant there was a decreased chance he would yell at me or the boys. His episodes of rage, though, were truly frightening. Not only would his voice be raised, but his face would be inches from mine and his natural light blue eyes would turn a menacing solid black. It didn't take much for Ben to be set off like this and these rages, though at the time infrequent, began to make me think twice about saying anything in general to Ben.

After tucking the boys in their beds and saying our bedtime prayers, I would get ready for bed as well. One late night as I lay in bed, in the stillness and quiet of the dark, I closed my eyes to start up my last conversation with God for the day.

Seriously, God, where are You?! I feel so alone in this. Do You even hear my prayers? Don't You see the pain I'm in? I feel like You've deserted me and I'm dealing with Ben all on my own. Do You even care?

I have to admit, my prayers were raw. I brought my pain to God in the most honest way I could. There was seemingly nothing I could do to improve my situation, and I just wanted God to show me that He was still there with me in my struggle. I prayed for God to show me that He was near. And not only that, but I also specifically asked for Him to make it obvious, so I didn't miss anything. I desperately needed encouragement from God, and there was none to be found.

Or so I thought.

Every fall at church, our fresh-faced first graders were

given a Bible. This year we found ourselves in front of our congregation as Greg received his first Bible. He beamed with his trademark ear-to-ear smile as he hugged his new Bible while our pastor spoke about this special gift.

Later that evening, as I tucked Greg into bed, he asked if we could read from his new Bible. I was thrilled at the suggestion and enthusiastically exclaimed, "Of course we can!"

"So, which book of the Bible should we read?" I asked him as I flipped to Genesis, assuming it would be his answer.

Greg excitedly responded, "Let's read Exodus!" My dear second-born son, Greg, has always been a bit quirky, off the wall, and an out-of-the-box thinker, so his request didn't entirely surprise me.

"Why do you want to read Exodus?" I asked him curiously.

He nonchalantly said, "Oh, because in Sunday school today, we learned about Moses helping the Israelites escape."

"Ah, I see. That's an exciting story—wanna read it again?" I asked casually as I turned the pages to Exodus 14. Greg nodded with a big smile on his sweet face.

I began to read the story about Moses leading the Israelites out of Egypt and was moved when I got to the passage about how God protected the fleeing Israelites from Pharaoh and his strong army of men in chariots. As the Israelites fled, they looked back to see Pharaoh and his army coming after them. At that moment, the Israelites bitterly blamed Moses for their dire predicament. Trapped. Hopeless. Frustrated. I related easily to these emotions, as I had endured the same ones in this difficult season of my marriage. Then something amazing happened! God parted the waters and allowed the Israelites to escape on dry land. Oh, how I wished that God would rescue me from my disastrous situation as well. *God, please part these waters.* The verse that stood out to me as I read the story to Greg was Exodus 14:21: Then Moses stretched out his hand over the sea, and all that night the LORD drove the sea back with a strong east wind and turned it into dry land (NIV). I was reminded that God did the impossible and in their extreme circumstances, God provided safety and protection for the Israelites. Because God saved the Israelites from certain death, they learned to trust Him. It was an encouraging moment for me and a reminder that I needed to trust God in my circumstances as well. I wondered if this was God's way of showing me that He was indeed present in my marital chaos.

I finished the chapter, prayed with Greg, and kissed him goodnight. As I headed downstairs to complete my evening chores, I thanked God for the precious time I had shared with Greg. I had been praying for God to show me that He was still present in my situation. It was a timely message reading about the Israelites, and it gave me a bit of hope that maybe I wasn't as alone as I had previously thought. Maybe, just maybe, God *was* near me after all.

By the time I finished cleaning up the kitchen and catching up on some work on my computer, it was just past midnight. Still struck by the timeliness of reading Exodus 14, I decided that I needed to draw closer to God now more than ever. I usually like to do my quiet time in the morning, but since I felt this strong desire to be near God, I decided I'd read from one of my favorite apps. I tapped the Proverbs 31 Ministries app on my phone and was shocked to see that the highlighted verse of the day was the same exact verse that stood out to me from my reading with Greg–Exodus 14:21! Of the over 31,000 verses in the Bible, *this* was the theme verse?! I remembered that not only did I ask God to make

His presence known to me, but I also specifically prayed that He would make it obvious, and He did. To me, it was further confirmation that God heard me and reassured me that He was absolutely with me in my struggle. With renewed confidence that I wasn't alone, I headed up to bed, and I slept better that night than I had in many months.

THINGS GO FROM BAD TO WORSE

After my encounter with God that night, I had renewed hope. Maybe He will indeed rescue me as He did the Israelites. Strengthened by this new hope, I tried to be patient with Ben, waiting on God's cues to lead and give me direction. I decided to be more aware of how I lived my life, even if it meant going against Ben's wishes–something that I had avoided in the past as I tried to keep the waters calm.

Southern California is blessed with wonderful weather, which offered us numerous opportunities to enjoy our patio in the backyard. We often ate meals on the patio with views of the nearby hills, followed by s'mores by the fireplace. One evening, as we had dinner outside, Ben was playing DJ and selected his reggae playlist. I don't mind reggae myself, but I found some songs rather inappropriate for the kids. I decided to speak up and casually requested that we change the playlist.

Dumbfounded, Ben furrowed his brow and asked, "Why?"

By the way he asked that one word, coupled with the

look he had on his face, I knew this could go one of two very different ways. He would either brush it off casually and change the playlist as I had requested, or my response would ignite yet another one of his explosive rages. Unfortunately, it was the latter. Since I decided recently that I would do the right thing even if it meant upsetting Ben, I grounded myself internally and responded to his question. "Well, the kids are a bit older now, and I don't want them exposed to these lyrics."

That's all it took.

In the past, we had kept these rage-filled moments away from the kids. I soon realized this was not to be one of those moments. While our young family sat at the patio table, Ben immediately launched into a profanity-laced tirade about how uptight I was and that it's really not a big deal. I calmly picked up my plate and left the table, thinking that it would be safest to excuse myself. Ben abruptly rose from the table, and I heard him stomping furiously behind me, his footsteps getting louder as he approached.

The second he entered the house, he started yelling at me about my mental health, that I needed help, that there was something wrong with me, and that I needed to seek therapy. *Wait... what?!* As he went off on me, I was fixated on how twisted his view was. I had simply disagreed with his musical choice for the sake of our young kids, and he was telling me that I need to get help for my mental issues. It didn't make any sense to me.

When he finished his lecture, he stormed back to the yard, sat back at the table with the kids, and acted like nothing happened. I was shaken to see how quickly his demeanor had changed in mere seconds.

I began to wonder if what I had just experienced was a red flag for me to leave Ben. *God, are you allowing situations to tell me to get out?* I couldn't reconcile the commitment I made in our marriage vows with a message that seemed to be from God. Again, it simply didn't make sense. On these occasions where I tried to sort out my situation, I secretly wished Ben would make it easy for me. If he did become physically violent or if he were to have an extramarital affair, I'd have my "get out of jail free" card. I'd have a convenient and justifiable reason to file for divorce. But because I was in neither of these two situations, I banished the thought.

Now that these explosive moments were occurring more frequently, I felt more and more stuck in my marriage. The daily stress of dealing with Ben began to take a toll on my physical health as I realized I was more anxious and felt like I was entering depression. These symptoms were to be the first of many.

I NEED A PROFESSIONAL OPINION

"Do you smell that?" I asked Ryan.

Ryan took a big whiff of air, paused, and responded, "Smell what? I don't smell anything." He looked at me quizzically.

I scrunched up my nose. "That smoky smell. It's really strong."

The first time I smelled smoke, I brushed it off, assuming it was in the air and everyone else was similarly affected. It was an odd event, though, as I started to smell smoke more regularly and in areas I didn't expect it, like in my living room or in the car when I was alone. The smell of smoke, similar to that of cigarettes, was so intense that it was as if I was in a nightclub. At times, the foul odor was strong enough to cause me to cough, to the point of making it difficult to speak.

I began to worry as the smoky smell increased in both intensity and duration. Concerned, I knew I had to see a doctor about it, but of course, I consulted Dr. Google first. Upon a quick online search, I learned that what I was experiencing was called phantosmia, a phantom smell. These olfactory hallucinations can be attributed to various medical conditions, including the presence of a brain tumor, depression, migraines, or seizure disorders (Weil, 2017).

Soon after completing this research, I made an appointment to meet with a neurologist. He ordered an MRI to rule out a brain tumor. The results showed that there was no tumor, much to our relief. The neurologist then asked some questions about my mental health and asked if I might be depressed. It was very possible given the stress I was under at home. I agreed that my usual happy-go-lucky persona was replaced by bouts of anxiety and dread. He recommended I meet with a psychiatrist to explore this further.

I made an appointment to meet with Dr. Narendra, a psychiatrist that Ben had seen in the past. As we sat down, I explained my symptoms and what I was going through at home. From our discussion, Dr. Narendra diagnosed me with situational depression because of the constant stress I was under and offered a prescription for a low-dose antidepressant. Situational depression is a type of depression that occurs in the short term due to stress (Cirino, 2018). The doctor expressed concern for my general health, knowing that medication wasn't going to be a permanent fix for the challenges in my home life.

"Sydney, you can't be under stress like this for the long term. Perhaps the olfactory hallucination of smoke is your body's way of warning you that you're in a dangerous situation. You will likely bring on more physical ailments as time goes on. You need to leave Ben."

"Wait, what? I don't leave relationships. My most meaningful relationships are decades old. It's just something I don't do." It was preposterous to me, at the time, that the option to leave my marriage was spoken with such nonchalance.

Dr. Narendra continued, "Well, you can choose to stay with him, but if you do, please know that by the time you're in your eighties, you'll be a shell of the person you are today."

The doctor's words startled me. She had a valid point—I understood her genuine concern, and it made sense to me that I shouldn't allow the potential for additional illnesses to arise because of chronic stress. But I was committed to my marriage, and I wasn't going to leave so easily. I prayed about her advice and decided that I would make an appointment to meet with a Christian therapist. Surely someone with a faith perspective would be able to suggest a better alternative for me.

A few weeks later, as I sat in Gary's comfortable office—a Christian therapist I'd discovered through my network—I started to explain why we were meeting. I shared about my previous test results and appointments from both the neurologist and the psychiatrist. Glancing up every now and then, Gary quietly noted in his legal pad all that I was sharing. He wanted to know more about my relationship with Ben. I didn't hold anything back and told him about the confusing behavior I've encountered: the rages, the criticism, the lack of emotion in tragic situations, acting like he made all the rules, yet the rules didn't apply to him. I shared particular disturbing events related to these behaviors. I told Gary that I had no idea what was going on, but I felt like I was going crazy. He put his pen down and point-blank said, "Your husband is a narcissist."

"A...*what*?" When I think of the word narcissist, I think of Narcissus of Greek mythology—the character who fell in love with his own image. That's not quite how I saw Ben.

"A narcissist. You're dealing with a narcissist here." Gary went on to explain the typical characteristics of a narcissist: self-importance, fantasies of perfection, feeling special, having a need for praise, entitlement, manipulation, lack of empathy, jealousy, and arrogance (Raypole, 2021). As he mentioned these traits one by one, I was able to connect specific events related to specific symptoms. I was relieved to know that this was a "thing," that I wasn't simply imagining these moments.

"You need to leave him, even if it's temporary. You need to leave him."

What? I did not expect to hear that from a Christian therapist. "What do you mean?" I asked, astounded by how conclusive Gary's recommendation was.

"Here's the thing. You have three little boys at home, and they're watching and learning from Ben. He's showing these boys that this is how a husband treats his wife and how a father treats his sons. You cannot expose your sons to this and let Ben be an example to them. This will continue to the next generation if the boys adopt this behavior as normal. You're in an abusive situation."

Wow. This whole time I was so focused on juggling everything with my marriage, thinking I was adequately shielding my young boys from Ben. The very thought that my little guys might repeat this behavior horrified me.

As I left Gary's office, I was relieved that I now had an answer to what I was experiencing but also frightened at the prospect that I might have to seriously consider what both Gary and Dr. Narendra had strongly recommended–leaving Ben.

Later that night, when all was still and quiet, I sat in front of my laptop and started to research narcissists. I was taken aback that so many others were going through what I was going through. I had felt incredibly alone for so long, thinking my situation was unique. I recalled that Gary referred to my home life as an abusive situation. As bad as things were, it never crossed my mind that what I was experiencing was abuse. I always equated abuse with physical violence, but that night, as I learned about narcissism, I also learned about narcissistic abuse. What I had been experiencing was verbal and emotional abuse from my narcissist husband. It was incredibly validating to learn that I wasn't imagining things.

Never one to jump into a hasty decision, I brought it to the Lord. *OK, God, here we are again. I'm so confused about what I should do. Do I leave as the professionals think I should? Do I stay and try to honor my marital vows? God, if it's Your will that I should leave, please make it obvious to me.* I prayed that, not knowing what to expect. Neither option felt right. Leaving didn't feel right. Staying didn't feel right. Armed with my new perspective from the mental health experts, this was to be my prayer for the next six months.

THE DECISION TO LEAVE

In April 2014, during the boys' spring break, Ben and I decided to take our family on a road trip to Northern California. Married life at home was challenging, at best, and we needed a change of scenery. We tailored our weeklong itinerary with each family member's interests in mind. For the boys, we planned visits to the children's museum in Santa Barbara, the world-famous Monterey Bay Aquarium, the Ghirardelli Chocolate Factory in San Francisco, and historic Sacramento. We would visit two of Ben's favorite breweries in Santa Rosa, and I would visit my familiar wineries in Napa. Along the route we mapped out, we would also visit Merissa and her family in San Francisco and some dear friends in Auburn before making our way home.

Even though family vacations are meant to be fun-filled and a time to unwind, for most moms with young kids, it can often be a stressful time because they're still on duty and mom-ing— which is even more complicated without the familiar conveniences of their own homes and schedules. I understood this, but I was determined to create some lasting memories for our family, tempering my expectations with knowledge of the unpredictability of Ben's behavior. As we had seen in Hawaii, Ben had a track record of ruining vacations.

Ben took the week off from work and looked forward to all that we had planned. We started our adventure early one morning after packing the minivan. Before heading out, he led our family in prayer for a safe trip, and with each boy excitedly anchored in his car seat, we began the long drive. As we took off, armed with snacks, cozy blankets, and various quiet activities, I silently prayed for a peaceful time with Ben, asking God to direct my interactions with him.

Those first three days were truly wonderful. It brought me such joy to watch the boys interact with the hands-on exhibits at the children's museum, stare in wonder at the amazing sea creatures at the aquarium, and hunt for sea glass at the beach. They were having so much fun with each other and I appreciated this break from their usual fighting. Even Ben seemed at ease as he bonded with the boys over decadent chocolate desserts, awe-inspiring landscapes, and funny stories from his own childhood. I recall being surprised that the trip was going much smoother than I had anticipated.

Of course, this was only the first half of the trip. What was to follow in the second half was nothing short of disastrous.

Next on the itinerary was a visit to one of Ben's favorite breweries in Santa Rosa. We parked the car, and I offered to drive so he could enjoy a few pints of his much-loved microbrew. Ben excitedly walked ahead with Ryan while I followed behind with the two younger boys. As we approached the crosswalk, I noticed that the "walk" sign had changed to a blinking "don't walk." It was still a few seconds before we would arrive to cross the busy intersection, meaning that by the time we did arrive, the signal would indicate "don't walk." I suggested we wait, knowing I had the two slow-walking younger boys in tow. I was shocked by Ben's reaction to my seemingly innocuous comment. "Oh, c'mon, Syd, stop being so uptight and let's cross already! It's not a big deal."

It might not have been a "big deal" to him, but as a mom looking out for her children's safety as well as trying to teach them to follow basic rules, it actually *was* a big deal. Ben's sour disposition continued as we entered the brewery. It was a busy afternoon, and there weren't any available tables. In a huff, impatient, and disappointed that he wouldn't get to have his anticipated pint, Ben grumbled, "Forget it–let's just go then."

This was the turning point of our trip.

It was a quiet drive to the hotel. I opted for silence, not knowing how anything, however harmless it may be, might set off Ben. We finally arrived at the hotel, and after a long day, we had a quick dinner and went to bed without further incident. Perhaps tomorrow would be a better day.

The boys woke up excited, ready for another day of fun. It was a bit early, so I let Ben sleep in while the boys and I explored the hotel grounds. We returned in the late morning only to find Ben still asleep. The boys were looking forward to visiting the *Peanuts* exhibits at the Charles M. Schulz Museum. By the time Ben woke up and got ready, the museum had closed for the day. Disappointed, Ryan lamented, "How come Papa only wakes up early for his things and not ours?" I didn't have an answer that wouldn't paint Ben in a negative light, so I distracted Ryan, reminding him of the other fun things we had planned for the rest of the day.

Ben's temperament for the second half of the trip was a stark contrast from the first half. He was becoming irritated with the boys and was constantly on them for trivial matters. We still had another three days to go, so I tried to balance Ben's bitter behavior and the boys' excitement. For the next day or so, we were generally able to tread water and keep the peace.

At one of our final dinners on the trip, we decided to dine at a nicer restaurant. One of Ben's biggest pet peeves was having dinner interrupted because one of the boys must use the restroom. Knowing this, he asked the boys to wash up and use the restroom soon after we placed our dinner order. The kitchen was slammed, and it took quite a while for our meals to arrive. Just as the server placed the food on the table, Greg announced that he had to use the restroom. Ben immediately went into a tirade: "I told you to go before dinner! Now you're just going to have to sit and finish your dinner. You can go after dinner."

Knowing little seven-year-old Greg with his little seven-year-old bladder was not going to be able to make it through dinner, I offered, "Go ahead and start without us; I'll take Greg."

Thinking that my offer was a favor to Ben and that he would appreciate the gesture, I was surprised by his body language when I returned to the table. As he sat across from me, he glared at me with stone-cold eyes. I was confused by his behavior but carried on as my food was starting to cool. He didn't utter a word for the remainder of the meal while the boys and I ate and chatted. Something was definitely off with Ben, but I couldn't figure it out.

We made our way up to our hotel room after dinner, the boys eager to dig into the massive chocolate Easter eggs they had received as gifts from my brother-in-law's family earlier in the day. Ben walked ahead of the family, unlocked the door, and held the door open for the boys to enter. He then closed the door behind them, leaving the two of us alone in the hotel hallway. As soon as I heard the door click shut, I braced myself, knowing that what would come next was likely going to be another lecture. Even then, I was not prepared for the vitriol he was to spew.

"How dare you go against what I said at dinner! I told Greg to eat his dinner and you went against my wishes and took him to the bathroom," he started.

Two sentences in and this conversation was already ridiculous. "Listen, I was doing *you* a favor so that you could still enjoy your meal. I was not about to eat my dinner knowing that my son is uncomfortable," I shot back.

That I would even counter what he had begun was too much, and Ben completely lost it. With his face inches from mine, he called me just about every foul name I've ever heard in my thirty-nine-year existence. Beyond that, I honestly can't recall the substance behind his words–it's all a blur. It was at this defining moment that I checked out. I checked out of our conversation, I checked out of our vacation, and I checked out of our marriage. My hands and feet felt numb as the blood rushed from my extremities to my face. I could see his lips moving, his angry eyes with solid black pupils, the hate that emanated from him. I don't know how long it lasted, but after he got it all out of his system, he aggressively pulled out the card key from his pocket, unlocked the door, and walked in, casually asking the boys, "Hey guys, how are the chocolate eggs?"

Like nothing had just happened in the hallway.

I was done.

God, I'm SO done. I'm going to just take this as Your red flag for me to get out. I can't go on living like this. Even if this is not Your red flag, I'm tapping out because I just can't take any more of this treatment.

When we returned from our trip, I decided that the mental health counselors I met with were right. I had to leave Ben.

MY INDEPENDENCE DAY

After our dreadful spring break trip, I began to put together a general plan to leave. I couldn't take it any longer and decided to tell Ben that we needed to spend some time apart. I planned to have this uncomfortable discussion after the kids were out of school for summer as we didn't have our usual rigid commitments to tend to. I shared my plan with Danielle and, having recently completed her home renovation, she graciously offered us a place to stay after we left.

Even though Danielle and her family lived a short twenty-minute drive from our home, we often had them over for "framily" (friends + family) staycations. Three-day weekends meant opportunities for us to hang out and leisurely catch up. We would share a home-cooked dinner, Ben fixed fun adult beverages, and the five kids often created some sort of musical performance, painstakingly choreographed by Danielle's older daughter, London. We ended our evenings with dessert in our jammies, and when the kids and dads were off to bed, Danielle and I would get to enjoy some peaceful conversation. The following morning, we would work together in the kitchen, throwing together some sort of breakfast casserole or the like for our two families. This Independence Day weekend was no different. Except that, unbeknownst to Ben, it was to be our last.

Danielle and her family arrived in the late afternoon on the Fourth of July. London and her younger sister, Tiegan, clad in red, white, and blue stars and stripes, greeted us with excited smiles when we opened the front door. Since it was summer, we planned to grill and watch the festivities and fireworks from our backyard. Ben, charming as ever, doted on the girls and was a spectacular host to Danielle and Frank. I nervously went through all the usual motions of entertaining our dear friends, knowing that in less than twenty-four hours, life would change dramatically for all of us.

The following morning, after breakfast, Danielle and her family packed up and prepared to leave. As we said our goodbyes, Danielle's eyes locked on mine. She mouthed "text me" and I quickly nodded. Danielle knew that I was about to tell Ben that I needed a break from him.

The moment I'd both looked forward to and dreaded was finally upon us. When I saw Ben in the office by himself, I said a quick prayer and approached him.

"Hey, can I talk to you for a second?"

"Sure. What's up?"

"You know how I don't like taking pills? I'd really like to get off this antidepressant medication. I think we need to address the root of my depression," I started. "It's our marriage—we need to make some major changes."

I took a quick pause to steady myself, not knowing what would come next.

Surprisingly, Ben agreed. "Yes, I think we need to do something about our marriage, too."

Encouraged by his response, I continued, "I think we should see a marriage counselor to get us past this–whatever it is that we're struggling with."

Ben nodded in agreement. It was strange for him to be this amicable. "Yes, we should see someone to talk about our problems. We need to find out what's wrong with you."

There it was. He was pinning the failure of our marriage squarely on me. That was the reason he was willing to attend counseling. I ignored that bit so that I could continue with what I had mentally prepared in my head all these weeks prior.

"And while we're seeing a counselor, I think we should be apart."

"What do you mean? I don't get why we would have to be apart."

Ben wasn't able to see it from my point of view, and I felt my heartbeat quicken as I knew I had to be firm. He was not going to like what I was about to say.

"Ben, the last thing I want to do is to go to therapy with you and then come home and hear more of it from you, without the therapist present."

Things started to heat up as Ben insisted that we didn't need to be apart.

I explained that I'd already made up my mind and that this was non-negotiable. I turned and started to walk away to pack. Ben was on my heels, taunting me. "Oh, where ya gonna go? You gonna go to Mommy's house?"

"It doesn't matter where I am–I just need to be away from you!" I shot back, jamming random clothes into my backpack.

I should have been more prepared, but for some reason, I thought I would have time to gather my things. I grabbed my backpack, packing some clothes and toiletries. Ben was still nearby, mocking me, but I couldn't hear a word of what he was saying. I was focused on packing up the boys next. Having done so, I made my way downstairs. Amidst the commotion, the boys were keeping busy in the playroom. I quickly walked by and told them to get into the car. Still in their pajamas from the lazy morning, they obliged and hopped into the minivan. I threw our belongings into the trunk and slammed the door shut. Ben yelled, "Fine, then! Leave! Nobody's going to want you. Have a good life!"

But right before we left, Ben asked Ryan to come back into the house for a brief conversation. When he returned, I pulled out of the driveway and asked Ryan what Ben said. He responded, "Papa said 'tell Mama to come home.'" Those words bounced right off me, and I continued driving.

Our nation had celebrated its independence the day before. That day, I celebrated mine.

LOVE BOMBS AWAY

I glanced up at my rear-view mirror, seeing my past life behind me. The house, the neighborhood, Ben–I felt a sense of sudden relief knowing that I had finally taken a firm stand, but now I faced the uncertainty of the future for the boys and me.

Knowing that thinking too far ahead would only overwhelm me, I needed to concentrate on the immediate next steps. *OK, I just need to get to Danielle's house.* I texted her on the way informing her that we'd be there soon and that I'd catch her up.

The intensity of our sudden departure was broken when one of the boys piped up, "Mama, where are we going?"

I quickly answered, "We're going to Auntie Danielle's house right now."

The boys didn't care about why we were going to Danielle's; they were simply excited knowing where we were headed. Danielle's house had always been a place of refuge for me, but for the boys, it meant a place of non-stop fun. Hanging out with Danielle's daughters, who may as well have been their sisters, munching on late-night snacks, and splashing around at the neighborhood pool were a guaranteed carefree time.

When we arrived, London, the ringleader of the five kids, took charge and shuttled the boys off to play. Danielle and I went upstairs to chat in private and I caught her up on what had just happened with Ben. The reality of it all hit me, and I burst into tears. I was overwhelmed by the gravity of the situation and how it would affect all our lives. She grabbed a box of tissue as I regaled the drama that had unfolded in the previous hour. Alternating between sharing what was going on in my head, shedding tears, pondering where we go from here, and moments of silence, I was in her room for what felt like forever. Danielle was surprised that Ben did not immediately come to her house to demand my return. Surely, he must have known where I would be. Danielle left me alone for a bit to collect myself while she ordered pizza for dinner.

After a quick dinner, the boys washed up and got ready for bed. I had intended to settle them down and wanted to chat further with Danielle and Frank, but I was emotionally drained from the day's distress and quickly fell asleep instead.

The next morning, I woke up with a crying hangover headache. *Did yesterday really happen? Am I finally free from Ben?* I reached out to my close friend, Anna, who was a marriage and family therapist. I told her that I had left Ben, and she was genuinely shocked. Anna never suspected we had any issues in our marriage because to the outside world, Ben exuded charm, stability, intelligence, and care. She didn't even know the monster behind the mask existed. From Anna's professional experience, she wanted me to be aware of a few things. She warned me that in the coming days and weeks, he would "love bomb" me by turning on the charm and showering me with apologies, flowers, and promises, and that I should be aware that these would be attempts to lure me home. After a brief honeymoon period, there was a very good chance that things would revert to the life I was fleeing.

Since we had left for Danielle's in such a hurry, the boys and I needed to pick up a few things from the store. As we were checking out of Target, I ran into one of my church friends, Bethany. She greeted me with her typical Bethany warmth and asked what we were doing in town. I briefly shared that we had just left Ben, and we were trying to figure things out. She was shocked, and I knew I had to fill in the blanks so that she understood what was going on. Obviously, catching up at the end of our Target run didn't allow me enough time to explain everything in detail. Bethany asked what I was doing later that afternoon and invited me and the boys over so that they could play with her kids, and we could chat over tea. She later told me that she was just at Target without plans to shop and left the store empty-handed. I've never left Target empty-handed before, so I am convinced that God placed Bethany in my path that day for a reason! Time with Bethany is always refreshing for me, and after updating her on all that I was going through in my marriage, she prayed over me and my situation. She would be the first of many friends to lift us up in prayer.

It was difficult to decide who needed to know what was going on at this time. I did know that I had to notify my best friend from high school, Susan. She was aware that we were going through a rough time in our marriage but didn't know that I finally decided to leave Ben. With my permission, Susan contacted Ben to inform him that she and her husband, Jay, want to assist us in any way they could in resolving the situation. He thanked her for her offer but never took her up on it.

I had planned to visit Merissa in San Francisco with the boys several weeks earlier, having already decided to leave Ben. I felt that being hundreds of miles away from Ben for a while would be a welcome distraction for us all. Sure enough, Anna was spot on. During our visit, Ben sent two huge bouquets of my favorite tulips to Merissa's apartment, apologized for how he treated me, and made promises to change. Ben expressed what appeared to be genuine remorse for his actions and agreed to see his psychiatrist, promising of returning to his bipolar depression medication.

I commended him on making this commitment but told him that I would need more time apart. Ben had never demonstrated that he could control his behavior for more than two weeks, and I wanted to ensure that I waited at least this period of time to monitor his behavior. Ben understood and was open to the idea that I needed this time. I was optimistic but guarded in my expectations. Only time would tell if he was sincere about his promises.

ABRUPT REGRESSION

.

A fter our quick trip to San Francisco, we returned to Danielle's house. We were hosting Vacation Bible School (VBS) at our church that week and I was signed up to serve. The boys were excited to attend this annual summer tradition with their friends. It had been two weeks since I left Ben and during those fourteen days, he made a point to reach out by phone or text daily as an attempt to right his past wrongs. One day, he asked to have lunch with the boys because he missed them. It was never my intention to keep the boys from their father, so I gladly dropped them off at his work so that they could spend some time together. They were excited to see Ben, and lunch went off without a hitch.

In the past two weeks, Ben had been diligent about responding to all my calls, texts, and emails. I was hopeful but still cautious about his renewed commitment to improve his behavior. We kept in touch during the week of VBS and I invited Ben to join us for the closing performance at the end of the week as the boys would be participating. It was odd that my invitation was not acknowledged. *Hmm...maybe he forgot to respond.* A day later, I reached out to him once more. And again, no response. I became concerned by his lack of communication, but with the VBS performance coming up, I was busy with preparations and tried not to read too much into it. I told myself that if Ben showed up, great. If not, I would realize that things had taken a turn for the worse. It was strange that we had been communicating so regularly, but now it was radio silence.

The night of the performance arrived, and Ryan asked if Ben would attend. I told him that I did invite him, but that I didn't know if he'd be able to make it. We'd just have to wait and see. My poor boys' faces fell when Ben was not in the crowd of attendees later that evening. It was clear to me at this point that Ben's two weeks of good behavior had expired.

Then, Ben went on the offensive and drastically changed his behavior towards me–again. He decided that everything was now my fault. He accused me of being ungrateful for all that he had done for our family. He claimed that my behavior caused him to turn to drinking as he had in previous years.

It was precisely the possibility of this change that had kept me from returning when he had requested. With this new development, I had to alter my game plan and protect myself, not knowing what Ben was capable of.

FOUR WALLS DON'T MAKE
A HOME

S ummer began to draw to a close with no improvement in our marriage. I was disappointed that Ben continued to ignore me and made no attempts to seek professional help as he had previously promised. Despite our strained dynamic with Ben, though, the boys and I lived a carefree summer. Knowing our family life was filled with friction and instability, I did my best to keep the boys happy and occupied with friends and activities: day trips to Newport Beach, night swimming at the neighborhood pool, spending time with their grandparents, and camping in the Sequoias.

After spending almost two months with Danielle's family, reality hit, and with school reopening in a few weeks, I had to make important decisions about our living arrangements. To keep things as stable as possible for my sons, I decided that we would move back to our hometown so the boys could continue at their schools with familiar friends and teachers. The idea of returning to life under the same roof as Ben was enough to cause me anxiety, so I decided that it would be best for us to live apart while we figured things out. To my relief, Ben agreed.

I found an apartment down the street from our family home and thought it would be ideal because Ben would be only thirty seconds away from the boys. He could see them whenever he wanted because of our proximity. I was nervous about living in such close quarters with neighbors, though, knowing how loud my boys could get. I asked God to help us find an apartment that might be suitable not just for me and my unpredictably noisy boys, but also for our future neighbors.

With school just around the corner, I visited the apartment complex closest to our house to see what units might be available with our timing. I described to the apartment manager what an ideal apartment would be like for me and my boys: a two bedroom, two bath apartment, but ideally, an apartment with no shared walls and if possible, nobody above or below us. I wanted to be a considerate neighbor, but it seemed like a tall order, and the manager wasn't sure she would have any available units given our timing and specific requests. She kindly offered to take us on a tour of the property anyway and to show us what units were available, and which might work.

We toured a few units that met the basic requirements of the number of bedrooms and bathrooms, but the few available units that worked with our timing all had multiple shared walls. To me, multiple shared walls meant multiple neighbors affected by our noise. I thanked the apartment manager for the tour and prayed that God would help us find the right apartment soon.

Not knowing where we would live in a few weeks, I began to consider other nearby apartments and tried to find a creative solution for our housing situation. A few days went by, and the apartment manager called me saying that she had good news to share! One of the residents in one of their rare carriage house units just notified them that they had to vacate immediately, and the unit was a perfect fit. When we had visited the previous week, none of these carriage house units had been available to be shown and the apartment manager hadn't even cared to mention them as they were so rarely available. I learned that the carriage house unit had two bedrooms, two baths, and no shared walls. Furthermore, the unit had no neighbors below because it was located above a row of garages, and it had no neighbors above, either. I saw this opportunity as something orchestrated by God knowing that there were so many factors involved regarding specific requests, availability, and timing—none of which were within my control. All I could do was praise God for providing for our family as He did.

I was thrilled to have a place for just the boys and me. Friends offered to babysit, and I made plans to return home while Ben was at work to pack what I needed for our new apartment. My dear friends, Emily and Leah, offered to help me pack and get what I needed in order to settle in as quickly as possible. I was relieved not to have to pack alone–Emily and Leah kept me on track, and we were able to complete all of the necessary packing efficiently. It was easy to become distracted by the memories dredged up by specific items, and if they hadn't been with me, I would've dwelled upon memories or the "what could've beens." I packed suitcases and boxes with the boys' clothes and shoes, dishware, and the basic necessities to get us by. I told Ben I was taking the love seat, the folding table, and the folding chairs. I didn't care about moving all our furniture; instead, I focused on what we really needed: somewhere to eat, somewhere to sleep, and somewhere to sit.

Moving day arrived quickly, and we moved our boxes and limited furniture to the new apartment. As I stared across the apartment at the sea of boxes, I was overwhelmed, knowing we had to unpack everything and realizing it was now my job to turn this foreign environment into a home for us. The boys were ecstatic about our new apartment and ran around exploring it–which, due to its size, didn't take long. For the time being, I decided that Ryan and Greg would share a room and that I would share my room with Isaac, sleeping on a full-size mattress on the floor. I planned to eventually get a bunk bed so that the three boys could share a room and I could use my room as a bedroom and office.

The following morning, in the stillness of a new day, I made my coffee and felt the first pangs of guilt for moving the four of us from our spacious 3400-square-foot home into our cramped 900-square-foot apartment. *Was this really the best decision?*

When the boys finally woke up, we sat around the folding table to eat breakfast. I looked at my little guys–Isaac wriggling around in his creaky folding chair–and I was overcome with guilt. I asked the boys if they were okay being here for a little while.

Ryan perked up, shot me a quick grin, and answered without hesitation, "I love it here, Mama!"

"You *do*?! I mean, we came from a much bigger house to this tiny apartment. You guys have to share a room with each other. You don't have all your toys. You really like it here?"

"Yeah!"

I had to ask why he was so quick to answer and when I

did, he responded, "I won't get yelled at for dumb things here."

At that moment, I was confident that the move was indeed the right thing to do. Ryan felt exactly as I did. Being in our tiny new home didn't matter because we were now free to do and say as we wanted without fear of reprimand– no more walking on eggshells. Home was truly defined by *who* we were with, not by the structure in which we lived. God had provided this apartment in such a timely manner, and my son felt at home–I knew we were on the right track.

BUT, GOD, I DON'T WANT TO
MEET WITH A LAWYER

My good friend, Sarah, texted me one day to check in. She was aware of our marital situation and asked to go for a walk to catch up. Sarah has always been in tip-top shape and as we hiked up the hill, she asked me how things were going with Ben. Huffing and puffing and trying not to sound as out of breath as I actually was, I caught her up on the last few weeks. I told her that I don't know where our marriage was headed and that I was losing hope by the day. She stopped me at the top of the hill (I was thankful for the break) and asked me, "But, Syd, what if this is the most amazing testimony for Ben? What if all this draws him closer to God?" Later, whenever I was ready to give up on marriage, I would ponder those words. What if Sarah was right?

Now that we were in separate dwellings, I was much more at ease. It was a relief from the chaos. Well, with the exception of the boys' fighting, of course. It was natural for them to have some sibling rivalry with brothers only two years apart. I accepted this as normal and intervened only when necessary. There was never a shortage of things to fight about–Legos, who ate the last popsicle, or who got to sit where on the couch.

Ben had purchased a new flat screen television for us when we first moved into the apartment. I sent him a quick email thanking him and telling him that while we were figuring things out, he could see the boys whenever he wanted–as long as he let me know so I could get it on my calendar. I offered this because for the entire first month we were in our new apartment, he never once asked to see the boys. His response to my thank you email was surprising, even to me. He quickly responded, "Of course, I know I can see the boys whenever I want. Do you know how many people have told me to lawyer up?!"

I was not expecting such a response. Interestingly enough, until this point, the thought of legal representation had never crossed my mind. I was still trying earnestly to work on our marriage, despite all the negative and withdrawn interactions Ben and I had had in the previous weeks. *Should I meet with a lawyer?* I briefly considered it but didn't feel it was necessary.

The next few weeks changed my mind. Maybe I was too trusting, or maybe I was naive, or maybe I just didn't want to think about it, but I honestly didn't think Ben would handle our finances any differently than he had in the past. I realized, however, that the potential for financial disaster was a very real possibility, and I prayed about what I needed to do to protect myself. I felt that it was probably time for me to consider speaking with an attorney to get some guidance. I reached out to friends and asked if anyone had a family law attorney to recommend. Anna responded and gave me the contact information of a lawyer she knew. I reluctantly picked up my phone, dialed the lawyer's number, and requested an initial consultation.

A few weeks later, I found myself in the parking lot of the attorney's office. *How did I get here?* I never expected I'd be seeking advice from a family law attorney. Never. My stomach turned as I prayed. *God, I really don't want to meet with this lawyer.* It was surreal–I still held out hope that God would provide some kind of miracle in our marriage. As I walked up the stairs, each step feeling heavier, I just prayed that God would bring me peace during my consultation. I was jittery, absolutely torn between wanting reconciliation and wanting to protect myself from Ben. It was strange that both scenarios seemed ideal.

The receptionist invited me to have a seat while she notified the attorney of my arrival. After a few moments, an immaculately dressed woman with short dark hair approached me and warmly smiled as she introduced herself, "Hi, I'm Megan." Her smile alone put me at ease, and I felt some of my anxiety melt away. We walked to her nearby office and exchanged pleasantries.

We chatted for a bit after sitting down, and when there was a break in our conversation, Megan asked, "So, how can I help you?"

I proceeded to tell her about my current situation with Ben: where we were in our marriage, how things had spiraled into the present circumstances, my conflicting emotions of reconciliation and divorce, and most importantly, the reason for our meeting. "I just need to know what to do at this point. What does a person in my position need to do to protect herself?"

Megan shared about what I needed to look out for and what goes into legal separation. "You know, Sydney, to be honest, with all that you've shared, I can tell that you still care deeply about Ben. For now, I'd like for you to work on your marriage for the next six months."

Wait, what? Did she just turn *down* my case? I was taken aback by her recommendation. I'd never heard of an attorney turning down a case before!

Megan went on. "Work on what you can during this time. I would like to make one suggestion, though. Please print out a calendar and note all the times Ben sees the boys. Nothing fancy, just the amount of time he spends with them during his visits. If anything comes up in the next six months, get back in touch with me."

And with this single recommendation, we ended our meeting. I walked out of the office, still shocked that Megan didn't want to take my case. Perhaps God was both encouraging me to work on reconciliation and giving me the information I needed. As I walked back down the stairs to my car, I thanked God for His creative ways of providing for me. It was exciting to witness God's presence in these moments!

With Megan's encouragement to work on my marriage, I made a plan to be more proactive. I understood from my research that couple's counseling with a narcissist is often unproductive; but we have a God of miracles, so I wanted to at least give it a shot. I prayed about the possibility of meeting with a counselor and Ben. I mentioned it to him, and he was open to the idea. I'm guessing Ben agreed to therapy because he wanted someone to concur with his assessment of my mental health, just like he did when I had first suggested it in July.

In hindsight, I should have spent far more time looking for the right therapist. Instead, I found someone in my network who was available to meet with us on a Saturday. We booked the first weekend that the three of us were available.

That dreaded Saturday soon arrived. Ben and I have had limited and sporadic contact with each other in recent months. We were barely on speaking terms by the time our appointment rolled around. When our therapist, Claudia, finally arrived at the office and opened the door for us, we each slowly approached the couch and sat at extreme opposite ends. First, Claudia asked me what was going on with our marriage. I began to give her a bit of history and as I spoke, I was overcome with the sadness and reality of our failing relationship and began to cry. She held up her hand to stop me from speaking, turned to Ben, and asked, "How does seeing Sydney's pain affect you?"

I glanced over to the end of the couch to see his reaction. Ben didn't look over to me and just shrugged his shoulders. Completely unaffected by my tears, he responded, "She does this all the time." Claudia then asked Ben the same question she posed to me about where we were in our marriage. He told her that I was oversensitive and read too much into what he said, totally missing the point of how his behavior impacted me.

We soon wrapped up our appointment and as Ben left ahead of me, Claudia turned to me and said, "I'd save your money on couple's counseling. Ben needs to work on himself before we can meet again."

Seeing how that session was unproductive, but still desiring to be proactive in working at my marriage, I prayed about other means to work on myself for the time being. I had a lot to process after all the years of torment with Ben. I sought out a new therapist as I needed guidance and a safe place to share all of my jumbled thoughts. Anna introduced me to Jennifer, a Christian marriage and family therapist friend from her time in graduate school. Jennifer was exactly who I was looking for and each time we met, I walked away with a renewed sense of hope. I felt emboldened as I established new boundaries with Ben.

Ben was not as close to as many people as I was, but he respected and enjoyed his friendship with Bodie, one of our church members. I was glad that Ben had someone to talk to, and I trusted Bodie to be the voice of reason in his ear. Bodie suggested that we hold an intervention with our church's pastor, Mike, his wife Angelina, and Danielle and Frank to see how they could support us in our situation.

On a Sunday afternoon a few weeks later, we gathered at Pastor Mike's office. The seven of us entered and took our seats which had been arranged in a circle. As Mike opened our meeting with prayer, I was hopeful that our time would be productive. I hoped that Ben would finally see our situation with fresh eyes—under the trusted care of those in the room—and be convicted to seek the help he so desperately needed.

Ben and I took turns talking about where we were in our marriage. It was news to me when Ben shared just how happy he was. Not necessarily happy about our relationship, but happy, in general. I found that rather odd. *You mean you're happy coming home every evening to a quiet, empty, lonely house? Your kids aren't part of your everyday life...and you're "happy?"* I couldn't comprehend that in his version of reality, he was honestly happy as he claimed.

During our meeting, we covered various topics surrounding our strained marriage, from how unsafe I felt around Ben to Ben's mental health to how we still felt about each other. Ben insisted that he had never physically harmed me, and I wanted to believe he never would, but I couldn't. When he was calm, I never felt threatened. However, when he would go into one of his rages, I *did* fear for my safety. Because of what I said, Ben agreed to respect my personal space and promised never to enter my apartment again. We talked about Ben's mental health, and Mike suggested that I accompany him on his visits to Dr. Narendra so that we were all on the same page. Ben agreed it would be a good idea and said that we would set that up. Finally, despite everything that had happened recently, Ben expressed his love for me. But instead of declaring his love for *me*, he stated that he would always love me because I am the mother of his children.

At the conclusion of our meeting, Ben held my hand as our intervention team prayed over us. The last thing I wanted to do was to have any kind of physical interaction with Ben; holding his hand during that prayer made my skin crawl. Leaving the meeting, I felt conflicted about just how productive it had been. Yes, Ben agreed in front of others that he and I would go to the doctor together to make sure we were all on the same page and that he got the specific help he needed. And yes, he agreed that he would not enter my apartment. But did we accomplish anything that moved the needle toward reconciliation? I felt more frustrated and less hopeful than ever.

A few weeks later, Ben came over to my apartment to drop off the boys after a quick afternoon visit. He was enraged by their behavior and stormed in to complain about them. I calmly asked him to leave, but instead, he got into my face as he had in that hotel hallway, shouting, "I'll go wherever I want! Who do you think pays the rent for your apartment?"

"Okay, Ben, you'd better leave right now. I don't know what's going on with you, but you cannot behave like this!"

"I'm fine. Just so you know, Dr. Narendra said there is nothing wrong with me! I have it in writing!"

Within thirty seconds, Ben had gone against the two promises he made during our intervention: never entering my home and seeing Dr. Narendra together.

I can't say that I was all that surprised that Ben didn't keep up his end of the bargain to see Dr. Narendra with me. I was due for another check-up with the doctor myself, so I scheduled an appointment to meet with her. I also wanted to check in and have a discussion with her about Ben. I communicated to her that during our intervention with our pastor and friends, Ben had agreed to meet with her and me together and to resume his medications.

A few weeks later, I met with Dr. Narendra. "It was the weirdest thing. I was just cutting carrots in the kitchen as I prepared dinner and when the garage door under our apartment opened, I jumped and was instantly struck by fear."

"I'm not surprised," Dr. Narendra said. "With all that you've experienced with Ben, you have complex post-traumatic stress disorder, or cPTSD." She went on to explain that this was common among victims of narcissistic abuse and recommended that I mention this to Jennifer the next time I met with her. While Ben and I were still under the same roof, whenever the garage door opened signaling that he was home from work, I was on eggshells. My mind and body now reacted that same way despite our living apart. The garage door opening had become a trigger for me that I needed to address with Jennifer. In the meantime, Dr. Narendra prescribed anti-anxiety medication for me to have on hand in case things spiraled out of control.

We shifted from my mental health to Ben's. Dr. Narendra confirmed that she had met with Ben a few weeks prior and mentioned that she found it odd that he requested his medical records from her. From what I shared, she believed that he did have bipolar depression (II) and that he wasn't misdiagnosed as he had claimed. She said that she could only treat him based on the symptoms he shared with her. When she asked him particular questions, he knew what to say to sound "normal," and she could only record what he told her. Hence, her case notes on him made him seem like he did not suffer from any mental illnesses. He portrayed himself as mentally stable and wanted her notes to prove his case.

Even when Ben had sought Dr. Narendra's help when I first left him in July, he only told her that he was depressed. When patients with bipolar depression are treated for depression with a selective serotonin reuptake inhibitor (SSRI), there is a strong possibility that it could send them into a manic phase (Bhandari, 2005). It was critical for Ben to be treated with the right medication and unfortunately, in these circumstances, he did not have the proper medication. This would explain his abrupt regression at the end of VBS week in July. He *had* sought help for depression, but unfortunately, had not been completely honest with the doctor about his exact symptoms and was given medication that sent him into an aggressive manic phase.

Though exhibiting five of the nine traits necessary to diagnose a person with narcissistic personality disorder (NPD) by the *Diagnostic and Statistical Manual of Mental Disorders, Fifth Edition* (Brazier, 2020), Ben had never been formally diagnosed. However, as I continued to unpack my situation with Ben, I learned there is a high chance of comorbidity for NPD and bipolar depression (Sagman & Tohen, 2020). There is no medication to treat NPD directly, but medication treating bipolar depression has been shown to decrease the effects of NPD symptoms Ben exhibited (Dellwo, 2021).

Following my meeting with Dr. Narendra, I updated our intervention team, who were disappointed that Ben had not kept his word. I hoped that this incident demonstrated to others that Ben had a side that many people were simply unaware of. Our relationship grew more dismal by the day, and I had serious doubts that we would ever recover from where we were now.

GOD SIGHTINGS

*N*ow what? God, I'm really trying to be obedient over here. I could easily throw in the towel, but I need You to give me some direction. Do I keep working on my marriage? Do I file for legal separation? Do I file for divorce? Things with Ben just seem like they're steadily deteriorating with no end in sight. Please show me what You want me to do. I'm so desperate for Your guidance.

Prayers such as these were common for me. In my ongoing conversation with God, I pleaded with Him to guide me. I wanted to be obedient, but it was increasingly difficult having to deal with Ben. Nothing felt right–until God started to reveal Himself to me through my friends and one particular stranger. Through a series of God sightings, God made His presence known to me.

Ryan had never really taken an interest in music, but because he was required to play an instrument in the fifth grade, the entire family gathered to watch his orchestra performance. All dressed up in a white button-down shirt and a snazzy tie, Ryan sat with his fellow trumpeters and played his heart out. We found out later that he was just pretending to play! Regardless, we decided that we would celebrate the momentous occasion with a visit to Baskin-Robbins for some ice cream. As we walked up towards the store, I noticed the familiar face of an old friend whose family had had the same post-performance idea. I hadn't seen Serena in many months, if not years. She excitedly ran up to me, gave me a huge hug, and said, "We *have* to get together so I can catch you up!" With her husband nearby, she whispered, "God saved my marriage!" I knew Serena and her husband, Joshua, had been going through a rough patch in their marriage not too long ago, so I was thrilled to hear that they had turned a corner.

"That's fantastic! Yes, let's definitely get together so you can catch me up. I'll text you and we'll get something on the calendar." Before we even met up, I ran into Serena two more times around town. I hadn't seen Serena in months and in the span of just one week, I bumped into her on three separate occasions. Was God putting Serena in my direct path for a specific reason?

Over waffles and coffee at a local Hawaiian brunch spot a few weeks later, Serena shared about how bad things had gotten in her marriage. She saw no way out. In her desperation and pain, she cried out to God and for Him to soften Joshua's heart. Through her prayers, she felt a tug to redirect her prayers from praying for Joshua to praying for herself. Through counseling and prayer, God orchestrated reconciliation. I was amazed by her faith, by how she trusted God in her uncertainty, and by how He finally delivered her.

With Serena sharing what she did and knowing how bad

things had gotten for her and Joshua, I was hopeful that God could do the same for Ben and me. After all, if our mighty God could raise His son from the dead, surely healing our marriage was well within the realm of possibility, right?

With a renewed hope, I continued to pursue reconciliation. At this point, there was no definitive reason why I should want otherwise. As difficult and uncomfortable as things were with Ben, I still held out hope and took Serena's saved marriage as God's way of showing me that I should continue fighting for my own.

A few weeks after meeting Serena for brunch, our town held our annual community garage sale. Ben and I had decided that since things were not moving in a positive direction, we would sell our family home to take advantage of the seller's market. We decided what items we wanted to sell, and the original plan was that Ben would handle sales that day. However, when the boys found out about the garage sale, they too wanted to participate. I am always one to encourage entrepreneurship, so I reluctantly agreed with the caveat that they stay out of the way. The night before the event, we baked brownies for the boys to sell to hungry shoppers and to keep the boys out of the way of the actual sale.

The morning of the garage sale arrived, and the boys were excited to see how many brownies they'd be able to sell. I hadn't planned to attend, but with the boys' participation, I had no choice but to go and keep an eye on them. The sheer size of the community garage sale often attracted residents of nearby cities and by the time we arrived at the house, the street was bustling with neighbors from near and far.

I noticed a middle-aged woman speaking with Ben about one of our furniture pieces from the end of our driveway.

After their discussion, she made her way down the driveway and approached me at our brownie stand. With a big smile, she stuck out her hand and introduced herself. "Hi, I'm Julie. I was just speaking with Ben about the table." She cautiously continued, "He mentioned that you're selling your home and moving into two separate homes." Julie obviously understood that we were living apart.

I nodded. She went on, "Marriage is so tough. My husband and I have been married for fifteen years ourselves. There was a time when we hit a rough patch and had to seek counseling and that put us back on track."

"Yeah, we tried counseling ourselves, but it didn't help. The counselor really wants Ben to work on himself before we can attend counseling together, but he refuses to seek help."

"I'm sorry to hear that." She paused for a few seconds and as she turned to leave, she asked, "Can I give you a hug?"

I didn't feel like I could say 'no,' and as someone who really is not a touchy-feely person, I surprised even myself when I quickly responded, "Sure!"

As Julie leaned in to hug me, she asked, "Can I pray for you real quick?"

I was surprised at her offer as nothing in our conversation would lead her to know that I was a believer and said, "I would really appreciate prayer, thank you."

We were still hugging as Julie prayed for us, our marriage, and specifically for Ben to be open and sincere in receiving help from counseling. I thanked her after her "Amen," still surprised that this stranger would care to pray for me.

Soon Julie and I started to say our good-byes and I asked her if she lived in the area. Julie smiled and said, "Not really! I live in Orange, about 30 minutes away. I'm just visiting a friend today, and she suggested we check out the neighbor-hood garage sale. I'm glad I did!"

I was glad that she had too. Julie didn't realize that God would use her that day to bless me with her wisdom and support of prayer.

Another few weeks went by. One day, my good friend Sabine messaged me from New Zealand. She told me that she had woken up that morning with Ben on her heart. She prayed specifically for the Holy Spirit to work in Ben and for him to clearly understand what needed to change and why. I thanked her for sharing and for praying so specifically for Ben.

I began my chores a few hours later and since it was laundry day, I started gathering the boys' dirty clothes. Our washing machine was in a closet on the balcony of our apart-ment. When I opened the balcony door, I noticed the floor was littered with sticks. Sticks everywhere! In my mind, I immediately blamed the boys for the mess and wondered what antics they were up to on the balcony. I opened the washer, threw in their clothes and detergent, and turned the dial. As the machine started up, I heard a thunderous flut-tering sound that made me gasp.

I looked down and was startled to see a little gray bird sitting against the washing machine, staring back at me.

My heart still beating rapidly from this discovery, I texted Danielle and told her about my new feathery houseguest. Always quick to point it back to God, she responded, "Think it could be something from 'the Big Guy'?"

"Hmm...I don't know, but that bird gave me quite a fright and I'm still a bit shaken up!"

When I had finally collected myself, I started to wonder whether Danielle was onto something. What if this was sent from God? After some research, I learned that the bird was a mourning dove and that these doves mate for life. Furthermore, as we know from the Bible, doves symbolize the Holy Spirit. It was only a few hours earlier that I had received Sabine's message about waking up, thinking of Ben, and praying for the Holy Spirit to work within him.

I deduced that the sticks on my patio were there because the dove was hoping to build a nest on our balcony. The boys, always desperate for a pet, were thrilled to see the dove when they returned from school. They asked to keep it and I told them 'no,' and that this sweet bird had a mate nearby. As I said that, Ryan exclaimed, "Oh yeah, there he is!"

I turned around to find not one, but two doves on my balcony. From that moment on, we continued to see two doves around the apartment complex. If they weren't on our balcony, they were on the balcony opposite ours, staring at us. We would see them together walking in the parking lot, sitting atop our roof, and fluttering near our car. Doves came to be a symbol of God's presence to me and the boys, and they loved pointing them out to me.

One afternoon, I saw a pair of doves walking by our garage. I whipped out my phone, snapped a quick picture, and sent it to Sabine. I explained that it was a bit difficult to see in the image, but there were actually two doves in the shot—one hiding in the shadow. Sabine soon messaged back that we have to have faith that the one in shadow will want to be in the light, where it's warm. I appreciated the symbolism and encouragement from the doves and Sabine that day.

As a believer, it's hard to imagine that these events taken together were purely coincidental. First Serena's story. Then Julie from Orange. And lastly, Sabine reaching out to me. All within a span of three short weeks. I could only attribute these instances to God responding to my request for encouragement. God was giving me what I had prayed for, and I felt encouraged that He wanted me to continue working on my marriage. I saw these three women–Serena, Julie, and Sabine–as God's messengers telling me to press on.

GOD SENDS MORE
MESSENGERS

God sparked a new desire for my marriage after my interactions with Serena, Julie, and Sabine. I found myself praying more than ever. Taking a cue from Serena, I began to pray for myself and my own heart rather than praying for Ben to change. I prayed for patience, for discernment, for wisdom. I asked God to reveal to me what I needed, so I could tolerate the contentious interactions and for Him to protect me through it all.

God led me to verses in Scripture that picked me up on my lowest days. He pointed me to devotionals that spoke specifically to my circumstances. He continued to put friends in my path who were just the right people I needed. One morning as I created my to-do list for the day, I noted that I needed to call Anna to get some advice. The day slipped away from me but that same night, out of the blue, Anna reached out to me to check in! As I kept relying on God, I drew closer to Him and found He drew closer to me. It was His strength that I drew from when I was weak. I was thankful for how

God continued to provide for me in His unique and loving ways.

One day I was doing some accounting and noticed a sizable amount of money had been deducted from the joint account Ben and I shared. When I asked him about this, he brushed it off explaining that as we prepared to sell our home, he had some expenses surrounding the sale and that was what the money was for. The money had been withdrawn from our account in the form of a check paid out directly to him. I had insisted that all such transactions show a clear paper trail so that both of us could see where the money went. I wasn't satisfied with his explanation and because of the size of the withdrawal, I was concerned and decided to get back in touch with my attorney, Megan.

Sitting across from Megan at her office again, I caught her up with our situation. "Well, I gave it my best shot, Megan. I followed your advice and attempted to work it out with Ben. I'm still hoping for the best possible outcome, but I think it's best if we pursue legal separation at this time so I can protect myself. I just don't trust Ben with how he's handling our finances."

"I completely understand. I'm glad you were able to carefully evaluate your relationship over the last six months," Megan replied. "We're only going to pursue legal separation and work to protect your finances at this time. We want Ben to understand that, so there won't be any mention of support or custody in the filing."

I made one request: "Is there a way to make sure that when he's served, it will be discreet and won't cause him any embarrassment?"

"Yes, of course, we can do that. We'll serve him electronically. Not a problem," Megan assured me.

I walked out of Megan's office that day relieved that we were taking steps to protect my assets, but also guilty for even having to take this step. It was necessary, though, and I felt like I didn't have any other options.

With the wheels in motion for legal separation, I carried on still hoping that God would somehow intervene. I trusted God with my future, but I also had to be realistic. I envisioned what life would be like if we headed down this path of separation and potentially divorce. By that time, I'd been a stay-at-home mom for close to ten years. Now that the boys were a bit older and in elementary school, perhaps I should entertain the idea of returning to work. But what would that look like? My past positions had required me to travel and that wasn't going to be ideal as I raised my sons.

Okay, God, I've always been told to pray specifically. If it is Your will that I return to work, please help me find a job that will allow me to work from home, such as a sales position with flexible hours, no travel, no need to meet with clients in person, and no need to dress up.

I thought this list of prerequisites was quite a tall order, but this was a list for my ideal job. Talk about praying specific prayers! And wouldn't you know it? God delivered! I found an online job site that offered flexible positions, mostly in a telecommuting environment. Not only that, but one particular job posting stood out to me as it met all the specific requirements I had prayed about. Since God did His part, I had to do mine.

I applied for the position, and the human resources contact, Sandra, tempered my expectations saying that they only hired one percent of the people they interviewed. This actually took a lot of pressure off me, and I treated it as a practice interview. Sandra explained that since this was a remote position, they vetted their candidates more thoroughly than traditional companies, and I should expect multiple rounds of interviews. Surprisingly, I continued to advance through round after round of interviews. The process was long as I met with various members of the management team. It was a welcome distraction from the drama in my marriage.

As I sought counsel from various sources, a church member asked me, "What's your part in this?" *My part in this?* I was shocked at the question and disappointed that this member didn't fully comprehend what I was going through. I learned that unless someone had experienced abuse themselves, they could not understand what I was experiencing. I will never profess to being the perfect wife, but I was confident that I hadn't brought the abuse on myself.

Later that evening my mentor, Mabel, set up a phone meeting between the two of us and her good friend, Lillian. Mabel shared that Lillian was going through a very similar situation with her husband. What complicated things for Lillian ---was that her verbally and emotionally abusive husband was in church leadership. All day, "What's your part in it?" played on repeat in my head, and I couldn't stop thinking about the question. As much as I attempted to put it out of my mind, I kept asking myself, "Wait, *do* I have a part to play in this?" As soon as Lillian got on the call, without knowing what I was asked earlier in the day, she said, "I want you to know that you did *not* cause this." Her first words immediately put me at ease, and I was relieved and grateful for her understanding and support.

A few weeks later, Danielle shared that she had had an intensely disturbing nightmare. She had debated even telling me about it. In the dream, we were all at a church that wasn't our home church. Ben was around but not present in the main church scene, though two of his relatives were. One of the two relatives was a young, blond woman there at church with her boyfriend. The other woman was Asian with dark hair and dark skin. The Asian woman was speaking with Danielle about my situation. In the next room, it was dark, the mood was somber, and everyone was lying on the floor. Ben had killed all of them. Danielle and others went to search for Ben all over town–in the dark neighborhood, through houses, and grassy hilly areas–but were unable to locate him. Meanwhile, I was nowhere to be found.

The next scene flashed to a building. Danielle and her husband, Frank, were in the elevator and really happy. The elevator door opened and in the lobby, outside the building's glass door, people were pounding on the glass to get in. There was a bad guy in the lobby and Danielle was now banging on the door to get out. Frank was suddenly outside with everyone else. And with that, Danielle was startled awake.

Danielle found this dream extremely disturbing. What could it all mean? In previous months, she had shared that one of the women at her Bible study, Cindy, had the gift of prophecy. Knowing about Cindy's gift, she decided to ask what she thought about it all. When Danielle first approached her, Cindy responded by saying that she needed to pray before trying to interpret the dream. After a little while, Cindy reached out to Danielle.

"Is your friend Asian? Are they divorced?"

Danielle responded that I was Asian and that we weren't divorced, just estranged and living separately.

Cindy next asked, "Does he have a young blonde American girlfriend?"

"Eeek...not that we know of!" Danielle responded.

Cindy then shared her interpretation of Danielle's dream. "OK, so Ben probably has a younger American girlfriend. The Asian gal in your dream is your friend. Everyone being dead represents how this split has killed and hurt people around Ben. Sounds like he instigated this split. You being in glass is actually how your friend feels. Ben and Sydney were happy, and people wanted what she had, but the enemy has come in and now the table has turned. She wants out of her situation and wants what others have. She feels trapped and scared. So sad. Pray for her and be there for her. Give her good counsel from the Lord. I'm sure you're already doing all these things. God is clearly speaking to you!"

Danielle texted back, "Yes, people around Ben are hurt! And she does indeed feel trapped and scared! Everything you said makes total sense, except no girlfriend that we know of. Actually, my friend left Ben because of emotional abuse. Maybe he has a girlfriend by now. Anyway, I've been with her through this whole journey and have shared a lot about our Bible study group to her. I'll let her know what God gave you about this. Thank you so much, Cindy!"

A few weeks later, Danielle let me know that Cindy reached back out to her. "Hey, does your friend have black hair, a bob cut, parted to the side?"

When Danielle confirmed that I did, Cindy responded, "That's what I thought! I had a vision last Thursday and just thought of it now that it's her. God knows."

A few days later, my phone buzzed, and when I looked down, I saw a text from Danielle. "Hey, would you ever consider meeting with my prophetic prayer friend from Bible study?"

I was rather apprehensive when Danielle proposed this

because I didn't know or understand much about prophetic prayer, but I figured I should keep an open mind in how I receive whatever help is available to me. As long as it was in line with my faith, Scripture, and of sound doctrine, I allowed myself to at least hear what Cindy had to share.

Danielle set up a time for us to meet at her house and we gathered upstairs to pray. Cindy and I chatted briefly as we walked up the stairs. Cindy didn't know much about me, with the exception of Danielle's disclosure that I was in a difficult marriage, that Ben and I were not living together at the time, and the bits and pieces Cindy had interpreted from Danielle's dream.

We took a seat on the plush couches and settled in. "This might sound weird, but I'm being led to place my hand on your heart as I pray. Would you be comfortable with that?" Cindy asked.

Danielle snickered and quipped, "Ha, Syd loves that!" knowing how I shy away from others when it comes to people touching me.

"Sure, that's fine," I answered Cindy, glancing over to Danielle and giving her a knowing smile. As Danielle anticipated, I was terribly awkward about Cindy placing her hand on my heart as she prayed. For once, I willingly took myself out of my comfort zone.

Since this was a new experience for me, I was nervous and excited about what would unfold. Cindy opened us in prayer and invited God to lead us. She would pray however the Spirit led. Alternating between silence and what came to mind, Cindy prayed with surprising accuracy about Ben's family history, his childhood with a negligent mother and an absent father, and the challenges that I was facing with Isaac's behavior at home. It was difficult to not become emotional with all that was being revealed to Cindy and to listen to her pray so specifically for the challenges I faced.

As we were getting ready to leave, Cindy asked, "Are you working right now?" I responded that I wasn't.

"I have this strong feeling that you're going to be very happy, very soon." And with that, Cindy said good-bye.

Cindy's final words to me almost made me discredit her gift of prophecy. She obviously didn't know the daily chaos I faced. How could I possibly be "very happy, very soon?" I dismissed this remark as my future was so dark and daunting. However, in a few weeks' time, I would realize that Cindy was right.

GOD RESCUES ME

"I'd like to walk Ryan to school on his last day of elementary school," Ben texted.

I responded, "Sure, that's fine. The promotion ceremony will start soon after drop-off."

Our necessary correspondence was brief, to the point, and free of any casual pleasantries. I let Ryan know that his father would be walking him to school. I was thrilled to see him walk the stage and promised to meet him after the promotion ceremony for photos. He was excited to finish his elementary school career and looked forward to all that middle school offered–which, from my understanding, meant much better cafeteria food.

I sat next to a friend in the auditorium waiting for the ceremony to start. I leaned over and whispered, "Hey, can you take a quick look around to see where Ben's sitting?"

She agreed, casually stood up, looked around the room, and sat back down saying, "You know, I don't see him anywhere."

How strange—he was just here. Maybe he stepped out for a bit.

One by one, students approached the microphone, said their name, walked across the stage, and were handed their promotion certificates. When it was Ryan's turn, something funny happened. He walked up to the mic, slowed down, and mumbled his name quickly. As he walked away, the principal motioned for him to repeat his name because he rushed it. We all had a good laugh over it.

After the ceremony, I was nervous about any kind of face-to-face interaction with Ben. Surprisingly, I still didn't see him. I approached Ryan and congratulated him on his accomplishment, and he flashed his mouthful-of-braces smile. I asked whether he had already taken photos with Ben, but Ryan said, "No, I didn't. He's not here."

"Are you sure? Papa just dropped you off."

"I'm sure, Mama. I was looking for him in the crowd but didn't see him anywhere. I saw you, Adam's parents, Mason's parents, all my friends' parents...but not Papa." He spoke bravely, but there was a tinge of disappointment in his voice.

Looking back on it, Ryan must've been right. If Ben had been there, he would have made some sort of comment about Ryan's principal asking him to repeat his name when he walked across the stage. It was heartbreaking to think that Ben had not made it a priority to be there for this milestone event.

A few days later, I found myself back at Megan's office. "I can't believe I'm doing this. Of all days, today." I took the pen from Megan, signed my name, and dated it June 3, 2015–Ben's birthday. The legal separation papers were prepared, signed, and dated. The following day, they would make their way through the appropriate channels.

"It's just a date; don't think too much about it," Megan assured me. "Once everything is processed, I'll let you know, and we'll take it from there."

Gone were the days where June meant celebrating Ben's birthday on some tropical international vacation. Instead, I was in my attorney's office signing papers for legal separation. Thinking back on how far we'd fallen saddened me, but I knew that this was something that had to be done for the welfare of my boys and me. I was slightly guilt-ridden signing his birth date on the documents. But in all honesty, at the rate we were going, I wished I was signing papers for divorce instead.

Since it was Ben's birthday, I wondered what the appropriate thing was to do. *Do I ignore his birthday entirely?* I wasn't about to buy him a present or even call him, but I figured a quick 'Happy 44th Birthday' text with appropriate emojis would be harmless. I texted him that I hope he had a good day without any expectation of a response. None came, and I was perfectly fine with it.

Three hours later, the doorbell rang. The man on the other side of the door asked, "Sydney Silver?" I wasn't expecting anyone and opened the door without thinking too much about it.

"Yes?"

Before I was able to ask any questions, the man handed me an envelope and said, "Consider yourself served. Have a good evening."

Whoa. Did that really just happen? Shocked but excited, I quickly opened the envelope. It was true. Ben had given himself a little birthday present in the form of a petition to dissolve our marriage.

In total disbelief, I grabbed my phone and hurriedly

texted Danielle, "I just got served dissolution of marriage papers by Ben!!! Happy birthday to him! Call me when you get out of your women's group."

Danielle immediately texted back, "Is that divorce? Can't talk...but wow!"

"YES!"

An hour later Danielle texted again, "I cannot concentrate at women's group...had to sneak to the bathroom to text. Are you okay?"

"I'm fine, Danielle. This is totally God's protection over me, and I welcome it."

"I'm so glad you're okay. Then congratulations. God totally rewarded you for being obedient. Talk later!"

Ben had no idea I'd been to Megan's earlier that day. He had no idea I had been speaking with a lawyer. He had no idea I had signed papers for legal separation. He had no idea that I was secretly hoping for divorce. But God knew. He saw everything, and He gave me far more than I could bear to ask. I was amazed at God's timely rescue.

I recalled the countless times I had questioned if leaving Ben was the right thing to do. When staying seemed both right and wrong. I began to realize that God had been providing for me in ways that I never could have imagined. These moments assured me that God was moving mountains on my behalf and providing for me in His creative ways.

In the previous months, I had prayed for Ben to find God through this mess. Sarah's voice echoed in my head as I remembered her asking me, "What if this becomes the most amazing testimony for Ben?" I texted Sarah to inform her of the latest development, which was Ben's desire to pursue divorce, and how I had been served papers mere hours after signing off to begin the legal separation proceedings.

Sarah was as shocked as I was that this happened and shared that she felt God was stepping in at just the right moment. She compared it to Abraham, who, in great faith and obedience to God, was about to sacrifice his son Isaac when God intervened. I always appreciate when my friends point at these moments and bring it back to God. Sarah recognized how badly I wanted to divorce Ben, but at the time, it just hadn't felt right, so I had chosen legal separation.

For most women, being served divorce papers would most likely be construed as a negative event. In my situation it was quite the opposite. I saw this as one step closer to being officially free of Ben's clutches, and it brought me great relief. Knowing Ben's character, I understood that despite welcoming the divorce, the months ahead would likely be painful as we started to untangle the life we'd created.

GOD PROVIDES

For weeks after Ben's birthday, I was still in disbelief that God had rescued me as He did. Megan and I met to discuss the necessary paperwork. My head spun as she asked for all sorts of documentation. I was intimidated at the prospect of gathering all that Megan requested as Ben handled our taxes and finances.

During this time, I was nearing the end of the interview process with Sandra. I had successfully completed my final interview with the company's founder and CEO. Things were progressing well, and I began to feel confident that I would be offered the position.

I met up with Megan again to review the paperwork. Now that we were moving towards divorce, we had to calculate what custody time and financial support might look like. I was thankful that Megan had told me to track the number of hours Ben spent with the boys. We had roughly eight months of data showing Ben's visitation time and after Megan ran the numbers, she was shocked to learn that the boys were with me 97% of the time. I expected this outcome as Ben rarely saw the boys and for the entire month of May, he didn't come to see them–not even once. After reviewing the documents from Ben's attorney, Megan calculated the financial support. I was comfortable with her calculations and figured it would allow me enough time to get back on my feet.

As I settled into bed that evening, I thanked God for the initial estimations for support. These numbers were higher than I had anticipated, and it made me wonder whether I even needed to pursue the full-time sales position that I had been interviewing for in the past two months. I didn't want to take away any more time from the boys than I had to, but I had come so far in the hiring process. It had been a long day and I figured I'd just spend time in prayer about it the next day.

After dropping the boys off at school, I poured myself a hot cup of coffee, sat in front of my laptop, and began checking my email. I wondered what I should do about the sales position. Imagine my surprise when I received an email from Sandra explaining that, due to internal restructuring, they had decided to scrap the full-time sales position I was interviewing for. Sandra said that they would like to bring me onboard, but for a part-time marketing position they thought I would be better suited for anyway. I confirmed with Sandra that I would be happy to join the team on a part-time basis. After a bit of back and forth, she was even able to offer me more than I had originally negotiated for my compensation. I would learn that this company was a blessing indeed. The remote work culture the company created emphasized such a positive environment, and I was given the chance to work with some of the best people in the field.

I hadn't even had time to bring this whole situation to God as I had planned, and He orchestrated something that was more fitting for me. Not only that, but when I remembered Sandra mentioning the low hiring rate of one percent of candidates interviewed, the fact that this was the only job I applied for and the only position for which I was offered an interview, the entire process was nothing short of miraculous. I did not attribute this to my own merit, having been out of the workforce for so long, but rather to God's providence. Between Ben surprising me with divorce papers and my new job, Cindy was spot-on. It had only been a few weeks since we had met for prayer and I had been skeptical of what she said, but here I was, "very happy, very soon."

I marveled at how God had walked with me through my journey so far. Worship songs brought me tremendous encouragement. It seemed that on multiple occasions, just when I would need some encouragement, one particular song would play on the radio. This song spoke to me in a deep way and served as a reminder of God's constant presence. One day as the boys and I were returning from a weekend trip, this particular song came on the radio. There's a part in the song that talks about how at times we can't find God in our story, and as I heard those words, I remember thinking, "It's been a little while since we've seen any doves." And just at that very moment, as I sped down the 405 freeway at 75 miles per hour, a dove flew across my windshield! *OK, God, I see you!* It was precisely these times that I was strengthened knowing that I was not in this alone. God constantly provided me with what I needed in the biggest and smallest of ways.

DID GOD JUST ANSWER MY PRAYER?

G od continued to wow us. We continued seeing doves
when we were out and about. The interesting thing
was that prior to Ben serving me divorce papers, we always
saw doves in pairs. Two on the rooftop. Two on the balcony.
Two walking in the parking lot side by side. I don't know if
they were the same doves, but there were always two
together. However, after I was served, we began seeing doves
individually. The boys were accustomed to seeing them in
pairs, so if they saw a lone dove, they would always look for
its mate. None could be found.

As we slogged through the divorce filings, Ben suddenly
insisted on spending more time with the boys. He specifically
asked to see them every other weekend. Megan explained that
we have to be careful how we interpret this. It may have
appeared that Ben wanted to step up and be the present
father I've prayed for all these years, but it was more likely
that his attorney recommended he do this, so he wouldn't
have to pay as much in child support. I didn't want to read

too much into it but was glad that he made any sort of effort to spend time with his sons.

Megan had to relocate to Texas around this time due to her husband's job, but before she left, she introduced me to Amy, a fellow family law attorney. As we transitioned, I met with both of them and was grateful for another brilliant lawyer to represent me. Though I was sad to end my time with Megan, Amy had a good working relationship with the judges in the family court system, and I was confident that she was a capable replacement.

Weekends were now more structured as Ben had regularly scheduled time with the boys. The boys would stay with him every other weekend from Friday evening until Sunday evening. This time without my boys gave me a little break to rest from the everyday busyness of life. Never one to allow me to feel alone and being the amazing friend that she is, Danielle extended a standing invitation to stay with her and her family on Ben's custody weekends. I treasured these weekends as they allowed me to recharge.

One Sunday after picking the boys up from the house, Ryan asked me an interesting question. "Mama, is it true that you're only spending so much time with us so that Papa has to pay you more money?"

I was not only surprised, but also disgusted by his question. "What?! That's absolutely *not* true!" I quickly answered. "Why would you ask me that?"

"Oh, because that's what Papa told me."

"Ryan, I can assure you that I'm spending time with you and your brothers because I *want* to. I made the conscious decision to sacrifice my career to stay home and take care of you shortly after you were born. I wasn't getting paid then to spend time with you," I explained.

There was so much I wanted to say about Ben at this moment, but I refrained. "Ryan, you know I don't say bad stuff about Papa to you..."

Before I could continue, Ryan interrupted me, snickering, "Yeah, but he says a lot of bad stuff about you!"

"Well, you know what? If he says all of this bad stuff about me and you *see* me do it then it's true, and I am indeed the horrible person that Papa claims I am. *But* if you don't see me doing what he says, you have to think about who is telling the truth."

Now that the boys were spending more time with Ben, I knew he was actively working on the smear campaign. He wanted to paint me in a negative light to win them over to his side. It was critical that the boys and I communicate openly so that they could confront me about any lies Ben was telling them about me. In the beginning of these custody swaps, I had to figure out how to navigate these interactions and be on guard for whatever Ben would be sending my way via the boys. I knew he'd take these moments to draw the boys away from me in an attempt to draw them closer to him. Parental alienation, in which the narcissist tries to drive a wedge between the kids and the healthy parent, was possible–even likely.

It was now fall, and we were deep into flag football season. Every Saturday the younger boys and I sat on the sidelines cheering on Ryan, our favorite running back. Ben had the game schedule, but it was hit or miss on whether or not he would turn up. He was at least there consistently when he had the boys for his custody weekends. It was awkward and uncomfortable, to say the least, when Ben would show up at the games. When he did attend the games, he would ignore me entirely and only interact with

Greg and Isaac, and truthfully, that was perfectly fine with me.

After one of the games, as I started packing up our gear, Ben approached me and asked, "Hey, can I talk to you for a sec?"

Not knowing what was to come next or what this conversation would be about, I answered cautiously, "Sure, what's going on?"

"Listen, I'm not doing well. I know I need help. I don't know what's going on with me, but I know you might. I really need your help to figure things out."

I was not expecting this at all. Ben sounded sincere, and I wholeheartedly hoped that he was, but having been burned so many times in the past by him and similar moments like these, I made a quick decision not to commit to anything and responded, "I'm really glad that you realize that you need help. I just don't know how much I can help you. I need to pray about it and get back to you."

"Thanks, I really appreciate it. I really hope that you'll be willing to help me."

Is this God answering my prayer? Is Ben going to finally seek help as we've been praying for all these years? Or is this just another ploy? I had hoped that Ben would hit rock bottom, realize that he needed help, understand just how much he had at stake to lose, and would earnestly make changes that would alter his path.

For the next several days, I ran our conversation through my head repeatedly. I prayed over it countless times. Having done so, I felt in my gut that God was guiding me on how to respond. I sent Ben an email three days after our conversation.

Hey, Ben, thanks for sharing what you did on Saturday.

I'm glad you've realized that you need help. I've prayed about this since our conversation, and I don't think I am the right person to help you directly through this. I can gather a small group of our friends to rally around you and to support you, but I'm not the person to fill this role myself. I will definitely be cheering you on from the sidelines and will be praying for you as you heal. Based on my research, I believe you may be suffering from one of the following illnesses or disorders: borderline personality disorder, narcissistic personality disorder, obsessive compulsive personality disorder, and/or bipolar depression. Again, I'm not an expert, but I've dealt with your symptoms for so many years, and they point to this list of possibilities. I hope this is a good starting point for you as you seek help from a professional.

I must've re-read that email a hundred times before hitting the 'send' button. I realized that the victim should not be the one to help the abuser, so I felt confident in stepping back from being directly involved in Ben's recovery. I wasn't sure how Ben would receive the message. I hoped he'd understand.

I sent the email off and notified Amy, just to keep her in the loop. I didn't expect Ben to respond, but he did—in his own way.

We were moving along in the divorce process and wanted to work with a mediator rather than heading straight into court. As we prepared for mediation, I detailed my desires for custody and support. It was very simple, I explained to Amy. I wasn't out to get Ben's every penny. I just wanted to be fair, claim what was rightfully mine, and split things accordingly. Amy agreed with me, prepared the necessary paperwork, and submitted the documents with all our numbers for our mediation meeting.

A week after I had sent the email to Ben, Amy told me she had received the statement from Ben's attorney for mediation. She attached the document for my review. I was blown away as I read how vicious he was against my character. One paragraph particularly enraged me. He stated that throughout our marriage, I berated him and accused him of having many mental illnesses. Ben then copied and pasted the list of illnesses I emailed him as a starting point for his seeking help. What was meant to help him was now being used against me! Disgusted, I immediately responded to Amy and explained this. She assured me that this particular document was meant for the mediator to understand how custody and support were to be arranged, that my character was not on trial here, and the mediator would likely see who he was dealing with when he compared Ben's paperwork to ours.

Disappointed, but not at all surprised by Ben's latest stunt, I realized I needed to adopt a more defensive posture and be prepared for the unexpected when we eventually went to mediation. I had been hopeful that Ben was earnest in seeking help, but it appeared that he was only soliciting what he could to shore up his legal strategy.

SCRIPTURE COMES ALIVE

I woke up one morning filled with joy, and I couldn't understand how this was possible. *What can I possibly be happy about? I'm going through a stressful divorce with an unpredictable soon-to-be ex-husband, my long-term financial outlook is dubious, Isaac's challenging behavioral issues have yet to be diagnosed, I'm concerned about how this divorce is impacting the kids....*The list seemed endless.

Yet here I was, waking with a smile. It didn't make any sense to me. Then I remembered Philippians 4:7.

And the peace of God, which surpasses all understanding, will guard your hearts and your minds in Christ Jesus.

- Philippians 4:7

Is this why I have this peace? I couldn't explain it any other way.

Being raised in a Christian home and having gone to church all my life, so much of Scripture was familiar to me. It wasn't until I found myself in these desperate moments going through the chaos of dealing with Ben that Scripture came alive. Familiar verses suddenly held new meaning. I learned to appreciate the weight behind the words I'd read and heard throughout my life. It's one thing to read the words on paper but something entirely different to feel them in my thirsty soul.

I was excited to share my new love for God's Word with the boys when we did our homework for Bible Study Fellowship (BSF). This was the first year that the boys and I were involved with BSF, and I was thrilled to share this experience with them. I got even more excited when I was able to see the Scripture we studied come alive in the challenges we faced.

When Ben found out I was taking the boys to BSF, he sent a message from his attorney to mine that he, not I, should be the one taking them. I had to respond through my attorney that it didn't make sense for Ben to take them to BSF as they weren't with Ben during the week to get their Bible study homework completed. Between the two of us, we spent an obscene amount of money sending these ridiculous and frivolous letters.

The only times I felt it was necessary to get my attorney involved was when it came to protecting my kids' physical safety. Whenever the boys returned from Ben's, they shared stories about their weekend. I paid close attention because I wanted to make sure they were safe in his care. On one occasion, Ryan shared that he forgot his football cleats at the house as they were leaving for the game. As they were already late, Ben went back into the house to get his cleats and shoved them in Ryan's face through the passenger window. When Amy confronted him about this, Ben denied it and said that he placed the cleats on Ryan's lap. Ryan immediately denied Ben's narrative–and I believed him over Ben. This was just one incident of gaslighting that we experienced.

It was moments like these that got my blood boiling. The mama bear in me roared to life. But God in His perfect timing led me to Bible verses in devotionals or from friends. I was reminded that I was not to avenge (Romans 12:19), that there was another in the fire (Daniel 3:24-25), and that the battle is the Lord's (2 Chronicles 2:15). It was through Scripture that I released my human emotions and depended on God's supernatural powers to settle me down.

One day as I was searching for a new passage to put on my dry erase board, I prayed that God would reveal an applicable verse to me. That same week three friends sent me the same passage from Isaiah!

> But now thus says the LORD, he who created you, O Jacob, he who formed you, O Israel: "Fear not, for I have redeemed you; I have called you by name, you are mine. When you pass through the waters, I will be with you; and through the rivers, they shall not overwhelm you; when you walk through fire you shall not be burned, and the flame shall not consume you.
>
> - Isaiah 43:1-2

As verses arose and came to life for me, I would write them in my journal, save them as a screensaver to my phone, or post them on my bulletin board. I needed these constant visual reminders to get me through these difficult times and it was during these times I learned to redirect my anger and frustration to focus on my faith and prayer life.

GOD EXPOSES BEN'S LIES

"Which dress should I get?" From the dressing room of one of my favorite stores, I texted Danielle and Leah a photo of three dresses hung on the door. Mediation was coming up in a couple of weeks and I had to buy a dress— not my favorite thing to do for a tomboy like me.

In addition to finding a dress that I would be least uncomfortable in, I had to prepare myself mentally for the meeting. Having reviewed Ben's declaration and all the lies he spoke of me, I wanted to err on the side of being overprepared rather than underprepared. I printed out old emails and texts just in case I needed to prove anything to the mediator. I indexed everything so that I would be able to refer to topics and examples quickly. When I told Amy about my preparation, she reminded me, "Syd, you're not on trial here. You're going to be fine."

Despite Amy's assurances that I wasn't on trial, it sure felt like I was, knowing Ben and his curveballs. I shared the uneasiness I felt going into this meeting with my good friend, Taylor, and she encouraged me to lean on Scripture. She suggested that I choose a couple of key verses to write on my legal pad so that I could easily glance down and be strengthened, if necessary. Taking Taylor's suggestion to heart, I wrote out Deuteronomy 31:6 on my notepad.

Be strong and courageous. Do not fear or be in dread of them, for it is the LORD your God who goes with you. He will not leave you or forsake you.

- Deuteronomy 31:6

As I nervously drove to the office to meet with Amy, Ben, his attorney, and the mediator, retired Judge Hughes, I prayed in the car that God would simply protect me. I didn't know what to expect or what it would be like to meet with the mediator. I just prayed that Judge Hughes would see through the lies Ben painted of me and be fair in his decisions.

I arrived early and entered a small office where Amy was already waiting for me. She reminded me that we were well-prepared for the meeting. As we were chatting, Judge Hughes entered the room and introduced himself, saying, "Oh, I heard about you!" I felt my eyes widen wondering what he meant, but a split second later, seeing him smile I realized he was joking. He must've read Ben's statement and already had an idea about what was to unfold that day.

Judge Hughes' face then became serious. "How do you feel about being in the same room as Ben?"

"Well, if he's having a good day, I don't mind. But if he's having a bad day, I can't stand being in the same room with him. I get heart palpitations."

"Not a problem. I want you to stay in this office and I'll

meet with Ben and the lawyers. We'll come and get you if we need your input for anything."

I trusted Amy to represent me, so I was happy that Judge Hughes decided to keep Ben and me apart. I already began to feel God answering my prayers for protection. I sat down at the small table and opened up my laptop so that I could get some work done. I noticed the giant white board on the wall and wrote out Isaiah 30:18.

> Therefore, the LORD waits to be gracious to you, and therefore he exalts himself to show mercy to you. For the LORD is a God of justice; blessed are all those who wait for him.

> - Isaiah 30:18

The morning continued quietly, with Amy stopping in a couple times to make sure I was still doing okay in the little office. She told me that as soon as Ben's attorney requested 50/50 custody, both she and the judge laughed out loud. Knowing how little time Ben spent with the boys prior to the divorce proceedings, Judge Hughes said 50/50 was not an option. We would generously offer 80/20, continuing with the kids alternating weekends with Ben.

Judge Hughes stopped by on a break to check in and see if I needed anything. After spending some time with Ben, he understood our situation and he requested for me to stay in the office the rest of the day–there was no need for me to interact with Ben. Before he left the office, he paused to read the verse on the whiteboard. He smiled as he left.

Soon it was time for lunch, and Amy and I ate in my office. As he was still working on our case, Judge Hughes went back and forth between my office and Ben's when he had questions and needed clarification. He shook his head, sighing, and said, "Every five minutes I'm having to talk Ben off the ledge. He's near tears." We invited him to take a break and join us for lunch, and he said he'd get a plate and return soon.

Judge Hughes sat down and, before taking a bite of his lunch, said, "You know, you should be commended. You're nothing like Ben's brief said you were."

Relieved, I thanked him for seeing the truth and said, "I'm not out to destroy Ben."

"You and I can say that all we want, but Ben is never going to agree."

After lunch, Amy and Judge Hughes reconvened with Ben and his attorney. The day was quickly coming to a close with us agreeing on custody time and monthly support. Furthermore, because Ben believed I should be making more money than the job I had just begun, he requested a vocational analysis, which we granted. In turn, we asked that he receive a psychological evaluation, seeing that his behavior was so unstable around me and the kids.

All in all, I was pleased with the day's outcome—not only from mediation, but also from my one simple request for protection, which God graciously fulfilled.

"BE PATIENT"

Pleased with the outcome of mediation, I couldn't wait for the divorce to be finalized. It was likely many months ahead, but as I planned for my future with my boys, now a family of four, I wanted to create as much stability for them as possible. Now that our old house was sold, I started considering a more permanent home for us and prayed that God would lead us to our next home.

We wouldn't need as large a house as we did before, but maybe just a little more room for the boys–perhaps a town-home. We quickly found a townhouse in our city, directly across from the neighborhood park. I fell in love with the open floor plan and spacious kitchen, but because it was a townhome, we would share a wall with one neighbor. The realtor assured us that there was double insulation, fireproof sheet rock, and air gaps between the homes that would make them soundproof. With this assurance, I was convinced that this was the home for us and made an offer. Our offer was quickly accepted, and we began making plans to move in a few months.

By this time, the boys had become accustomed to our custody schedule. They knew they would visit Ben every other weekend, but they couldn't keep track of which weekends were with me and which were with Ben. Every Friday before school, one of the boys would inevitably ask, "Are we here with you this weekend or with Papa?" When I'd answer that they were with me that weekend, they would cheer, and there would be big smiles all around. However, if I told the boys, "You're with Papa," the mood in the room would change. Shoulders would droop, and there would be loud sighs and groans. "Why do we have to keep going back there?" I explained that if I didn't send them over, I would get in trouble with the judge.

To Ben, the kids were an inconvenience. He refused to have their toiletries, clothes, or toys at his apartment. Every time the boys visited him, they had to pack for the weekend. The boys couldn't wrap their brains around this–they even had their toothbrushes and some clothes at Danielle's!

Each custody swap worried me because Ben was so cruel to the boys, and there was no shortage of drama on his weekends. Ben felt the need to be an extra firm disciplinarian because he thought I was too lax with the boys. On one occasion, Ryan slept in on a Saturday and missed breakfast. When he awoke, Ben refused to feed him because he was already done serving breakfast, so Ryan offered to prepare his own. Ben denied Ryan's request because he didn't want Ryan to make a mess in the kitchen. Several hours later, Ryan asked for something to eat while they were out, and Ben reluctantly bought him a burger at a fast food restaurant but told him that he had to go and sit and eat alone, and that Ben and the brothers would wait for him in the car. I visualized this scene playing out and it absolutely broke my heart.

I never liked the idea of giving Ryan and Greg electronic devices at such young ages, but because their phones were a way for them to communicate with me should an emergency arise, I allowed it. Neither Ben nor I prohibited our children from contacting the other parent. There was an instance when the boys were under Ben's care, and I received a disheartening text from Greg. Being my kid who had always marched to the beat of his own drum, Greg did things in his own timing. Greg texted that Ben called him an idiot because he took too long to put his shirt on while getting dressed. The childish name-calling affected Greg on a deeply emotional level as he was Ben's scapegoat.

After a while, I grew accustomed to how Ben mistreated the boys, but even then, I was not prepared for the text I received from Ryan that Thanksgiving. I was celebrating dinner with Merissa and her family and received a text from Ryan saying that he overheard Ben telling his sister, "Only seven more years and I don't have to deal with Ryan anymore." This crushed Ryan, who was not yet aware that legal custody age limits would take effect at eighteen.

It was always a joyous occasion to be reunited with the boys. I treasured the first glimpse I got of them at pick-up on Sunday evenings and was greeted with their warm hugs and huge smiles. However, with each interaction becoming more contentious, I pressed Amy to see if we could expedite the psychological evaluation for Ben. I was becoming increasingly concerned about how he was affecting the kids, knowing how he affected me. One thing I found to be odd was that on the weekends the boys went to visit Ben, when they returned, they were noticeably kinder to each other. There was a camaraderie that was not their normal. I realized that whatever they were going through at Ben's compelled them to stick together and protect one another. They were in the trenches together, and their bond continued when they returned home to me. Of course, it only lasted a day before they resumed their usual bickering, but it was a noticeable change from their usual interactions.

As time wore on, I became more frustrated as I wasn't able to shield my sons from Ben's wrath. I cried out to God that I was doing all I could to play fair as we worked on the divorce. I wasn't asking for more than what's mine, I was civil to Ben, and I just wanted the divorce to be over already. I needed to hear from God on what I needed to do to get through this.

I remembered in a past conversation with a friend that when she wanted to hear God's voice more clearly, she would fast. I had never fasted before but was very interested in learning more and decided to give it a try. For someone who lives to eat, fasting is not something that I would normally have considered. That day, I replaced my lunch with worship and prayer. During that time, I poured my heart out to God. I know He was already well aware of my circumstances, but I needed to know what my next steps should be. The Spirit led me to hear God's voice saying, "Be patient."

Be patient?! Haven't I been patient this whole time?

I wasn't sure what to make of this message but was satisfied knowing that I *had* heard God speak to me. I resolved to be patient. I didn't know how much more patient I could be with Ben and everything that we were going through, but recalled the old hymn that maybe there really was "no other way...but to trust and obey."

MORE CLARITY

God, I'm so frustrated with Ben... Be patient.
God, you won't believe what Ben just said to the kids... Be patient.

God, how am I supposed to go on co-parenting with Ben... Be patient.

Whenever I grew frustrated with Ben, God's words echoed in my brain. *What does being patient even mean?* I realized after much prayer that I needed to trust God in His timing. Throughout my journey, God had demonstrated how His timing was always impeccable and how He provided more than I could have imagined asking for. Hearing from specific friends at precisely the right time. Being served divorce papers when I was only hoping for legal separation–just hours after I had signed off on my paperwork. Doves appearing suddenly just as I pondered my situation. How could I not trust God after He had consistently shown me that His timing was always perfect?

My conversation with God continued. As difficult as

things were, when I reflected on all that had happened in the past year, I realized that God had shown me favor in the most difficult circumstances and that I had to depend on Him now more than ever. As things proceeded favorably, I took it as God's assurance that He was pleased with the decisions I had made thus far.

I had never experienced visions, but one day, an incredibly vivid image popped quickly into my head, then just as quickly disappeared. Danielle and I were in a morgue, and we were there to identify Ben's body. She came up on his left side, and I was on his right.

I suddenly realized that God was going to take Ben from us.

I promised God that, assuming the vision was from Him, I would be honorable to Ben—despite the torture he had put me through.

I didn't share my vision with others because it disturbed me and made me wonder if I had read too much into what I saw. Ben continued to bombard me with ridiculous accusations through his lawyer, and I began having panic attacks. I'd never had them before, but one night, sleeping over at Danielle's, I suddenly awoke. My heart felt like it was beating out of my chest, and as my eyes darted around the dark room, I couldn't figure out where I was. I had been to Danielle's house and slept in the same room countless times before, but for whatever reason, I was confused and couldn't figure out where I was. Panicking, I fumbled for my overnight bag, which contained my anti-anxiety medication. My physical health was still suffering—depression, PTSD, anxiety, and now panic attacks.

Once I settled down, I closed my eyes and called out to

God again. *How much longer am I supposed to endure this?* And once again, in the stillness of night, I once again heard God say, "Be patient."

UNEXPECTED EVENTS

Another Friday morning, and Ryan started another round of "Where are we this weekend?" I took a deep breath and quietly answered, "You're at Papa's."

Ryan immediately launched into what his heart was feeling, "Why do we have to keep going back there? All Papa does is ignore us. How old do I have to be when I can refuse to go over?"

As I did every other week, I explained that for the time being, until Ben's psychological evaluation was completed, the boys had to continue going to their father's place as we had agreed during mediation. I further explained that it would look really bad to the courts if I prevented Ben from spending time with the boys.

It was Good Friday, and the boys would spend Easter weekend with Ben. After school that afternoon, as we gathered up the boys' weekend gear to head over to Ben's, I received a call from an unfamiliar number. I ignored it but listened to the voicemail. It was from Ben's colleague, Aron, informing me that Ben was not doing well and had just checked into a nearby mental health facility. I returned his call, thanked him for notifying me of this new development, and asked him to keep me posted. I also asked Aron to inform Ben's doctors that he had access to a gun.

I let the boys know that there had been a change in plans and that they were now going to spend the weekend with me instead of with Ben. They didn't care why there was a change–they were just relieved they didn't have to go to Ben's.

We had a quick dinner and headed to church for Good Friday service. I shook my head as I sat down next to Danielle in the sanctuary. *How am I supposed to react to Ben's hospitalization? Am I supposed to visit him?* I could barely focus on our pastor's message as I went back and forth between visiting Ben and supporting him from afar.

After service, I told the boys that Ben was in the hospital and asked if they would like to visit him. Without hesitation, Ryan quickly responded, "No, he doesn't deserve it. Maybe this is God punishing Papa for being mean to us." After all that we had endured with Ben, I fully understood and respected Ryan's position. Since Ben had played me for a fool so many times before, I ultimately decided not to rush to visit him. Instead, I sent him a text saying that I was glad that he was seeking help and that I would be praying for him as he recovered.

The following day, I checked in with Aron, who explained that Ben would most likely be hospitalized until Sunday. Over the course of the weekend, Ben's condition seemed to have stabilized and he was cleared to return home on Sunday.

The boys and I continued with our traditional Easter

celebrations at church and dinner with Danielle's family and some of our church friends. I was relieved that Ben had received help and was able to return home, not knowing that within twenty-four hours, I would receive the phone call that would change our lives forever.

I'M NUMB

As Ryan and I sat on the couch, his sobs subsided as he accepted that Ben was no longer with us. It was getting late, so I advised him to get some rest. I told him he could sleep in my room, which made him feel better. After sending Ryan off to bed, I reached for my phone and quickly texted Danielle, "Hey, can you talk? I know it's late, but it's important." I was thankful that Danielle was as much a night owl as I was.

I thought I had gathered myself enough to relay the shocking news, but as soon as I got the first words out, I just lost it. I had kept my cool as I told Ryan what had happened, but with Danielle, I was more vulnerable, sobbing hysterically as I gave her all the information I knew. Always the voice of reason, Danielle took in the news and assured me that I had her full support for whatever I needed in the coming days and that we would process through everything together, as we had many times before.

After we hung up, I started locking up for the night. The house somehow felt quieter and lonelier than normal. I walked upstairs and got ready for bed, emotionally exhausted by the news and thinking about what came next. My brain was numb, my hands clammy. I quickly texted Emily and Taylor to get in touch with me as soon as they woke up. I was still in shock and disbelief as I lay in bed, recalling the events of the evening.

Is this real? Is Ben really gone? I remembered God telling me, "Be patient," and how I had had a feeling we were going to lose Ben. For some reason, I had envisioned Ben getting into an accident; I never considered that we would lose him to suicide. As prepared as I was for Ben's death, I was not prepared for the complexities that surrounded it.

I tried to sleep, but I was startled awake every few minutes. A slideshow of my life with Ben played on an endless loop: our college days in chemistry lab, eating up a storm in Singapore, our move to the Pacific Northwest, experiencing the arrival of each of our sons, birthday celebrations–so many memories of all our years together. I saw smiles and tears of joy, and I heard laughter–only positive memories, memories I hadn't recalled in years. My mind and body were finally exhausted, and I somehow drifted off to sleep.

Ding! I woke up to the sound of the first of countless text messages I would receive. It was Emily checking in. I updated her and learned that there was just no way to put it except by stating what had happened. After her initial shock, Emily immediately asked how she could help. She agreed to inform Ryan's school that he would be absent until further notice and offered to bring pizza by later, so I wouldn't have to worry about feeding the boys lunch.

Soon after Emily's texts, Taylor reached out inquiring about my cryptic late-night message. I shared the news once again, learning to brace myself for a reaction. She quickly offered her condolences and, like Emily, asked how she could help. I asked her to notify the younger boys' school that they would be absent for the foreseeable future, and she assured me that I didn't need to worry about any school-related details.

Lying in bed, staring at the ceiling, I debated whether I should get more sleep or get started on my day. I knew I had a long day ahead with my brother, Gus, flying in from San Francisco, and my parents coming over to support me and the kids. I decided that I should probably get up, so I would be ready for the boys when they woke. I made my way downstairs and sat on the couch, still in utter disbelief and washed in sadness for how Ben's life had ended so abruptly. The younger boys still didn't know about his passing, and I tried to figure out when to tell them.

Ryan was the first to wake up and when he came downstairs, I explained to him that we would tell the younger brothers together, as the police officer had suggested. Greg and Isaac soon made their way downstairs and met us in the living room. I nodded at Ryan, signaling that we needed to tell the brothers now.

"Hey guys, I need to tell you something that happened yesterday," I started. "I got a phone call from the police last night that Papa is no longer with us. He's in Heaven."

I braced myself, expecting the reaction that Ryan had had at the news. Instead, there was a deafening silence from both Greg and Isaac. Not a tear between the two of them. Ryan took their silence as their not understanding what happened and said, "You guys, Papa's dead!"

There was a brief moment of silence. Greg then said,

"Okay. Can I go play Legos now?" and left the room as Isaac returned to playing his video game.

I wasn't sure what to make of their lack of emotion, and their reaction reminded me that I needed to schedule a therapy session as soon as possible. I followed Greg upstairs as he went to play. Sitting on the floor with him as he built his Legos, I asked him how he felt about the news. My sweet nine-year-old looked up at me and responded simply, "The monster can't hurt us anymore." His words resonated with me, and I understood why he was so at peace with Ben's passing.

He was right. The monster couldn't hurt him, his brothers, or me anymore. Never again. With this realization, I, too, felt a sense of peace.

SURROUNDED BY LOVE

I returned downstairs and sat on the couch. I knew I was overdue for my morning caffeine fix, but the very thought of getting up to prepare a cup of coffee overwhelmed me. Instead, I mentally planned a phone tree of who I needed to notify about Ben's sudden passing.

Just then, the doorbell rang and interrupted my planning. I looked at my porch security camera and saw it was Taylor. I opened the door and had to chuckle as she stood there, a to-go cup of coffee in one hand and a baked rotisserie chicken in the other. She looked at me blankly and said, "I just don't know how to help you right now." I thanked her and told her the coffee she held in her hand was exactly what I needed.

Soon after Taylor's visit, Emily stopped by with pizza as she had promised. But she not only brought pizza, but also stocked our entire fridge for the week with all the staples and extra snacks for the boys. I was incredibly touched by my friends' quick generosity and thoughtfulness.

The next day, we met with the boys' therapist, Dr. Bea. I

had emailed her expressing my concern that the younger boys weren't fazed by the news of Ben's sudden passing. She found it odd as well, and we met with the intention of allowing them to share what they were feeling. Dr. Bea first met with the boys, then Ryan alone, then all four of us together. At the end of our two-hour session, she took me aside and said, "You know, after talking with the younger boys and knowing their history with Ben, I just don't think there was enough of a relationship for them to miss. This might be why they didn't react with tears after the news." I was shocked, saddened, and relieved all at the same time. I would learn later that the emotional scars from the *abuse* they received affected them deeper than did Ben's suicide, causing PTSD, anxiety, and depression.

In the days and weeks that followed, we were further blessed by the outpouring of love from every direction. My friends never allowed me to feel alone that first week, and I am forever thankful. Danielle called a short list of friends and became our family spokesperson so that I wasn't over-whelmed with calls. Susan came over just to comfort me and unpack what was swirling in my head. Gus visited from out of town and was a welcome distraction for the boys as he took them out to their favorite burger joint and spent time with them. Our church life group brought dinner and prayed over our family. Ryan's school sent cozy blankets and signed posters to comfort us, teachers dropped off donuts, my parents made sure we were well-fed, and friends came by to make sure we knew they were available for whatever we needed–and somehow, they weren't intrusive. Weeks later, the guys from church emptied and cleaned out Ben's apart-ment. Danielle went through his mail and belongings so that I didn't have to see anything that I might not be able to unsee. I was beyond grateful for our community and how well we were supported in practical ways.

Since Ben took his life two weeks from the time our divorce was to be finalized, I was still legally his wife and took on all the necessary administrative responsibilities following his death. I remembered the promise I made to God weeks before that if He was indeed taking Ben from us, I would be honorable to him in his memory. Despite all the pain he caused the boys and me, I ensured that everything was carried out as he would have wished: no cutting corners, every decision thoughtfully considered.

As I planned Ben's memorial, I learned that my grief was complicated. I was angry for how he had treated the boys and me in the latter years of our marriage, for how he made this his legacy in his death, but as I recalled our past discussions about our final wishes, it reminded me of the happier and healthier times in our relationship. I chose to focus on who Ben was before he was overcome by mental illness and clung to the sweet memories I had of the life we had built together.

GOD'S PRESENCE

I n order to give our out-of-town family and friends time to plan for travel, I decided to have Ben's memorial the following month. This gave me ample time to plan the logistics of both the scattering of Ben's ashes and the memorial service at a local church. After visiting a few churches, I decided on one church that had a beautiful sanctuary filled with natural light. It was serene and bright, and I felt that Ben would have been happy with the service being held there.

As logistics fell into place, I worked on my eulogy to honor Ben. *How am I supposed to honor a man who treated my sons and me so badly?* I remembered my promise to God that in his death, I would honor him despite the pain he caused. Friends reminded me that I didn't have to eulogize him if I didn't want to, and I didn't jump at the chance to speak in front of a large group of people. However, I felt it was important for my sons to see me in a position of strength to instill confidence in my leadership of our family.

I am a master procrastinator and put off writing the eulogy for as long as I could. Finally, one day, I just decided that it was something that had to be addressed sooner or later, so I might as well get it over with. The silence in the townhome was too much for me, so I grabbed my laptop and headed to the busy neighborhood coffee shop to work on Ben's eulogy.

Armed with hot fresh coffee and determination, I stared at the blank screen before me. I prayed that the Holy Spirit would guide my fingers to type out just what needed to be said as I toed the line between the reality of what we experienced and compassion for Ben's mental health challenges. He led me to briefly touch upon the pain he inflicted but primarily focus on our happier memories together. I was surprised that the words just flowed, and within ten minutes, the first draft was complete. I reread it and was satisfied that it reflected the honest and appropriate tone of our time with Ben.

The big weekend arrived a few weeks later. We planned to scatter Ben's ashes with close family and friends first, followed by the church memorial service the next day. As I prepared for the scattering, I put on my wedding ring, which I hadn't worn since Ben had served me with divorce papers. It was a typical warm and sunny Southern California afternoon, and we walked out onto the dock to board the boat. The solemn atmosphere was accented by warm greetings from family members whom we see far too infrequently.

The captain started up the boat and we slowly made our way through the canal to open water. The captain dropped the anchor, met us at the bow of the boat, and invited us to share our memories of Ben. One by one, our family and friends shared their happy moments with Ben: Merissa remembered the one Thanksgiving we competed to see who ate the most (complete with before and after dinner weigh-ins), his colleague spoke about Ben's leadership at work, Ben's sister shared about the close bond they enjoyed growing up together. I enjoyed hearing their stories about happier times.

After our sharing, the boys helped me scatter Ben's ashes. I removed my wedding ring for the last time, kissed it, and dropped it into the water. Each guest received a long-stemmed rose to release. Despite the pain Ben had inflicted on us, I felt closure and a sense of peace.

Because doves played an instrumental role in our journey, the boys and I wanted to release a dove during the ceremony. The captain opened the box that held our dove and Ryan, our family animal enthusiast, asked if he could be the one to release it. The captain walked Ryan to the side of the boat and transferred it carefully to him. We all watched intently as Ryan slowly uncurled his fingers. The dove immediately took flight. I was moved seeing this, as if Ben's spirit was now free, but then it turned around, headed directly back towards our boat, and circled overhead three times before finally departing. Ryan turned to me and said, "That's so cool! Did they train the bird to do that?" I just smiled and whispered, "Nope, that was totally a God thing."

We concluded the service with prayer. Our good friends from church sang "Amazing Grace" accompanied by the soothing sounds of guitar strings and water splashing against the boat as the captain revved up the engine, and we headed back to the dock.

The next morning was the memorial. The boys dressed up–two of them chose to wear old ties of Ben's, the ties over-sized on their small bodies. I looked out at the sea of faces and saw different phases of Ben's life represented–family from near and far, childhood friends, colleagues, church friends. It saddened me to think that with so many people who cared for Ben, none of us could save him from himself.

The service began with music carefully chosen by our dear friends Jason and Jade and was followed by Leah reading from Scripture. Ben's closest friend from childhood was the first to pay tribute to him. Next, he was eulogized by his oldest sister and then by his colleague. Finally, it was my turn.

Approaching the podium, I took a deep breath and prayed that I wouldn't stutter. I intentionally didn't wear my glasses so that the sea of faces in the sanctuary would be slightly blurry and less intimidating. I felt the weight of each word as I remembered Ben in his healthier days, before his narcissistic ways brought chaos into our home and lives. I spoke directly to my three sons and reminded them that their father's passing would not define them and that without a doubt, God would bring beauty from ashes. I thanked our community for how they had loved on us not only in the weeks since Ben's death, but also in the months and years prior through prayer and in countless tangible ways.

Pastor Mike spoke next. He addressed the hurt that Ben had been going through before taking his life, reminded us that there is help for those who are hurting, and shared the hope that we have in Christ to heal through these tough times. I appreciated how Pastor Mike didn't gloss over the manner in which Ben left us and thankful that he invited those who have yet to know Christ to learn more about him. After Pastor Mike spoke, we watched a slideshow of the short forty-four years of Ben's life and concluded the service with words of appreciation from our family.

The boys and I exited the sanctuary first to make our way to the reception in the next building. I was astounded by the food that had been set up and was so appreciative of my church family for handling the details. Soon friends met us in the reception hall and before I knew it, I was greeted and comforted by friends and family. One by one, they offered their condolences, gave the tightest hugs, and reminded me that they were covering our family in prayer. The outpouring of love was beyond anything I could've expected, and I was truly grateful.

That night as our family gathered for dinner, my father prayed over us and asked God to watch over the boys and me. It had been a long journey with the ups and downs of our marriage and family life, and as I sat at the table, I was strengthened by the love we had received in recent weeks. It was an emotionally draining day, so I decided to call it an early night. I was pleased with how we remembered Ben and grateful that God had enabled me to keep my promise to honor him in his memory.

I fell asleep quickly and slept soundly for the first time in many weeks. When I woke up the next morning, sun beams lit up my bedroom. A praise song ran through my brain and reminded me that this was the first day of my future. I felt joy and lightness after having laid Ben to rest. However, this joy would be short-lived as the coming weeks unfolded.

GOD CONFIRMS HIS RESCUE

I'm not sure if it was because of the flood of positive memories I'd recalled since Ben's death, but I found myself missing him in increasingly profound ways. For weeks after his memorial, I just couldn't shake the guilt I felt.

One night driving home in a rare Southern California rainstorm, I heard a song on the radio which spoke about always being there for a loved one, and I just lost it.

I wasn't there for him.

I should've done more.

I should've visited him in the hospital.

Why didn't I do more?!

All the should'ves, could'ves, and would'ves attacked me from every angle. Tears poured down my face as I was struck by this intense sadness. I wondered if I'd ever be able to forgive myself for what had transpired. *God, how am I going to get past this?* Well, God in His perfect timing would soon answer me.

Three days later, I received a text from Danielle. "Hey, your parents want to get together with us."

How odd. Why would Danielle be proposing a time to get together with my parents? Why didn't my parents ask me themselves?

I responded, "Why? What's this about?"

Danielle quickly texted back, "I think they'd prefer to be the ones to tell you."

Now I *really* became concerned. My intuition told me that my parents had discovered something while sorting through Ben's old files and documents. We arranged to meet at Danielle's house that night. My mind was swirling with all the unknowns and dreaded possibilities. *It has to be bad news. If it's good news, Danielle wouldn't have hesitated to share whatever information she had.*

Sitting at the dinner table that evening with Danielle and my parents, my dad opened the conversation by asking, "Who's Stephanie?"

I told him that she was an acquaintance and asked him why he wanted to know. As the story unfolded, I was first upset and angry, but those emotions soon melted away as relief took over. My father explained that while he and my mother were going through Ben's documents to sort out what I might need to keep, they had come across a set of printed emails that indicated that Ben violated his marital vows. It was surprising to me, but what was particularly interesting was that the emails pointed to these events taking place *prior* to me leaving Ben.

Throughout my difficult journey these past eight years with Ben, God showed His presence and rescue in timely and miraculous ways. Bible verses spoke loudly and clearly to me. God put the people He wanted me to speak with directly in my path. He showed me red flags to guide me to get out of my toxic marriage. Ben served me divorce papers just before I was to serve *him* with papers for legal separation.

And now this.

All of the guilt and intense sadness instantly evaporated as I realized that God was rescuing me from all that I didn't see–but He *did* see. As Cindy had told Danielle months ago, "God knows." God indeed knew what was going on behind the scenes and said, "Enough." I felt vindicated for the actions I was forced to take and for all the gut-wrenching decisions I had to make. The never-ending confusion of "should I stay or should I go" became a thing of the past as this revelation released me from all guilt.

One thing I was particularly aware of was the timing of this revelation. If my parents had told me about it before Ben's memorial, I know I wouldn't have been able to keep the promise I made to God just a month before to be honorable to Ben.

God is *so* good.

As I reflect on the last years of my marriage, I have come to realize that God truly rescued my boys and me. He forced me to leave and looking back, I now see all the pain we experienced as His protection. We didn't know it at the time through all the tears and swirling confusion, but God ultimately knew what was best for us. Romans 8:28 was a verse that my friends often shared with me on my most trying days.

> And we know that for those who love God all things work together for good, for those who are called according to his purpose.

- Romans 8:28

I have to admit that each time I was reminded of that verse, I would internally roll my eyes. *But you have NO idea what I'm going through! How can ANY of this be for "good"?!* It has taken me five years after Ben's passing to finally understand the pain I went through and ultimately, God's purpose for my life. I knew that I didn't want my story and experience to go to waste: I felt God nudging me to help other believers through the pain and conflicting emotions of being married to a narcissistic and abusive spouse. As we read in Scripture, He brings beauty from ashes.

God saw my pain. God knew my suffering. Even though the journey was rough, my faith and relationship with Him grew exponentially as I was forced to rely on someone outside of myself. God showed my sons and me His provision time and again, and I can now face uncertainty with confidence rather than worry. I'm thankful for how God creatively provided me with friends and loved ones who walked alongside me in my journey. I'm relieved that Ben didn't take the boys with him. I'm confident that everything I've had to go through will all be worth it in the end. I don't view the ending of my story as that–the end. Instead, I see it as very much the opposite and pray that you will similarly find that in your story as well.

The Beginning

GOD SIGHTINGS AND JOURNAL PROMPTS

Chapter 1 - Unknown Caller

GOD SIGHTINGS

- Despite horrific news, God is able to provide unexpected peace.
- This calm in the midst of confusion comes from knowing God.
- While the world is spinning out of control, God remains the same.
- God is the foundation and source of our stability.

SCRIPTURES

Psalm 62:2 He alone is my rock and my salvation, my fortress; I shall not be greatly shaken.

Isaiah 26:4 Trust in the Lord forever, for the Lord God is an everlasting rock.

John 14:27 Peace I leave with you; my peace I give to you. Not as the world gives do I give to you. Let not your hearts be troubled, neither let them be afraid.

JOURNAL PROMPTS

- Think of a time when your world came crashing down, what was your initial reaction?
- Did you turn to God, yourself, Scripture, or others?
- What helped you get through that specific moment in time?

STARTERS FOR YOUR PRAYERS

Look back at the above Scriptures. Write down the words that tell you God will give you peace. Now ask God to make those Scriptures more and more real to your life every day.

Chapter 2 - Happier Times

GOD SIGHTINGS

- Ben received medical help, an accurate diagnosis, and medication that worked.
- We had the opportunity to go to Seattle. We felt like we had God's blessing as Ben received

multiple calls from major companies and everything lined up so easily.

- Ben understood that he needed to change when the boys and I returned from Singapore.

SCRIPTURES

Matthew 6:31-33 Therefore do not be anxious, saying, 'What shall we eat?' or 'What shall we drink?' or 'What shall we wear?' For the Gentiles seek after all these things, and your heavenly Father knows that you need them all. But seek first the kingdom of God and his righteousness, and all these things will be added to you.

Philippians 4:6-7 Do not be anxious about anything, but in everything by prayer and supplication with thanksgiving let your requests be made known to God. And the peace of God, which surpasses all understanding, will guard your hearts and your minds in Christ Jesus.

1 Peter 5:6-7 Humble yourselves, therefore, under the mighty hand of God so that at the proper time he may exalt you, casting all your anxieties on him, because he cares for you.

JOURNAL PROMPTS

- Although you easily brush them aside, what were/are the little warnings that grew into unexpected, larger issues? Believe what you see. What do you actually see?

- Reflect upon something you and your husband prayed over and you saw God's clear leading.

Starters for Your Prayers

Consider the minor stressors in your marriage. Are there more serious underlying issues involved? Bring your concerns to the Father and ask Him for guidance.

~

Chapter 3 - The Simmer Begins

God Sightings

- Don't doubt what you feel and see.
- The Spirit of God gave me awareness of my situation.
- Realize your worth and that you don't deserve to be on the receiving end of abuse.

Scriptures

Proverbs 2:6 For the Lord gives wisdom; from his mouth come knowledge and understanding.

Proverbs 29:11 A fool gives full vent to his spirit, but a wise man quietly holds it back.

Proverbs 14:29 Whoever is slow to anger has great understanding, but he who has a hasty temper exalts folly.

JOURNAL PROMPTS

- In desperate times, it is critical to draw near to God. As we draw near to Him, He shows up in the most unexpected ways. What are some ways you can intentionally spend more time with God? (Some examples: studying God's Word, spending time in prayer, applying what you've learned from your time with God.)
- How can you commit to spending more time with God?

STARTERS FOR YOUR PRAYERS

Pray and ask God to give you awareness of your situation and for discernment in how you honor Him in your marriage.

Chapter 4 - The Penny Drops

GOD SIGHTINGS

- Friends helped me carry my burdens, encouraged me, and prayed for me. When I felt like I was fighting alone, it was a tremendous battle. Leaning on others gave me support and encouragement in unexpected ways.
- God led me to unknown resources I never considered previously.
- Actively seek wisdom from within your faith circle. Women at different stages of their lives

offer different perspectives from their own personal experiences and from their faith journey.

SCRIPTURES

Proverbs 18:24 A man of many companions may come to ruin, but there is a friend who sticks closer than a brother.

Ecclesiastes 4:12 And though a man might prevail against one who is alone, two will withstand him—a threefold cord is not quickly broken.

Proverbs 27:5-6 Better is open rebuke than hidden love. Faithful are the wounds of a friend; profuse are the kisses of an enemy.

JOURNAL PROMPTS

- Who are your supporters? Make a list of 5 people in your life who you feel comfortable sharing your private pain. Be mindful of who you include on this list as those who are not familiar with abuse and how it relates to faith might have a damaging effect on you. Meet with them and ask them to cover you in prayer.
- Of this group, select 2-3 who you know would drop everything to help you out at a moment's notice and reliably support you as you need.

STARTERS FOR YOUR PRAYERS

Thank God for the people He has placed in your life. If you can't think of any friends who will stick by you in your trial, ask God to bring someone into your life to walk through these tough times with you.

Chapter 5 - As You Wish

GOD SIGHTINGS

- Leah offered to do Bible study with me as an alternative.
- I received encouragement from my Bible study leaders to continue seeking God despite Ben thwarting my efforts.
- I appreciated the timely study about the Israelites and their journey through the wilderness. I saw many parallels with their story and mine.

SCRIPTURES

1 Chronicles 16:11 Seek the Lord and his strength; seek his presence continually!

Hebrews 13:7 Remember your leaders, those who spoke to you the word of God. Consider the outcome of their way of life and imitate their faith.

Romans 12:2 Do not be conformed to this world, but be transformed by the renewal of your mind, that by testing you may discern what is the will of God, what is good and acceptable and perfect.

Psalm 119:105 Your word is a lamp to my feet and a light to my path.

JOURNAL STARTERS

- Are you spending time in the Word as you go through your trials? If not, what can you do to commit to changing that?
- Is there a story in Scripture that reminds you of what you are currently experiencing? What truths can you lean on from the Word?

STARTERS FOR YOUR PRAYERS

Chances are that if you are married to a narcissist, he is likely extremely controlling. Ask God to help you brainstorm creative ideas around the narcissist's controlling ways. Draw your strength from Him.

∾

Chapter 6 - Encouragement from Afar

GOD SIGHTINGS

- My mom took away the pressure of staying in the marriage.

- As I walked on eggshells, God allowed me to recognize just how desperate my situation with Ben was.
- God used Greg to answer my prayer about showing me His presence when I was reminded of the Israelites' escape from slavery. Another confirmation from the Israelites' story came when my devotional's theme verse matched what Greg and I read.

SCRIPTURES

Romans 8:26 Likewise the Spirit helps us in our weakness. For we do not know what to pray for as we ought, but the Spirit himself intercedes for us with groanings too deep for words.

1 Peter 4:12-13 Beloved, do not be surprised at the fiery trial when it comes upon you to test you, as though something strange were happening to you. But rejoice insofar as you share Christ's sufferings, that you may also rejoice and be glad when his glory is revealed.

John 15:7 If you abide in me, and my words abide in you, ask whatever you wish, and it will be done for you.

Proverbs 8:17 I love those who love me, and those who seek me diligently find me.

JOURNAL PROMPTS

- What or who has encouraged you in your journey? How has their support affected you?
- Most women dealing with a narcissist husband find themselves walking on eggshells as I did. Consider the current situation in your marriage. In what ways can you relate?

STARTERS FOR YOUR PRAYERS

Consider the Israelites and their rescue from captivity. Pray that God will do the same for you.

~

Chapter 7 - Things Go from Bad to Worse

GOD SIGHTINGS

- I learned to depend more and more on God in both big and little ways. I was in constant conversation with God to help me with my daily life.
- God sustained me and helped me while I was in survival mode.
- Ben's behavior caused me to wonder if what I was experiencing were red flags from God.

SCRIPTURES

Micah 7:7 But as for me, I will look to the Lord; I will wait for the God of my salvation; my God will hear me.

Ephesians 4:29 Let no corrupting talk come out of your mouths, but only such as is good for building up, as fits the occasion, that it may give grace to those who hear.

Romans 5:3-4 Not only that, but we rejoice in our sufferings, knowing that suffering produces endurance, and endurance produces character, and character produces hope.

JOURNAL PROMPTS

- In what ways do you find yourself depending on God in your suffering?
- Self-care is essential when you find yourself in survival mode. In what ways can you practice self-care?

STARTERS FOR YOUR PRAYERS

Thank God for His sustenance. Communicate with God constantly so that your prayers are like an ongoing conversation with Him.

~

Chapter 8 - I Need a Professional Opinion

GOD SIGHTINGS

- God used the change in my physical health to spark conversations with medical professionals, ultimately helping me understand what's going on with Ben.
- God showed me that I wasn't imagining things and that there was a name to what I was experiencing.
- Hearing the same suggestion from both the psychiatrist and the Christian counselor made me realize that I needed to seriously consider their recommendation.

SCRIPTURES

Proverbs 2:10 For wisdom will come into your heart and knowledge will be pleasant to your soul...

James 1:5 If any of you lacks wisdom, let him ask God, who gives generously to all without reproach, and it will be given him.

Proverbs 3:6 In all your ways acknowledge him, and he will make straight your paths.

Psalm 73:26 My flesh and my heart may fail, but God is the strength of my heart and my portion forever.

Journal Prompts

- Reflect on your mental and physical health. Are you anxious or depressed? Have you experienced panic attacks? Do you need to speak with a therapist?
- If you need help but haven't sought counseling yet, what is preventing you from doing so? If you are in therapy, what have you learned and implemented?

Starters for Your Prayers

Thoughtfully evaluate your mental and physical health. If you are suffering, ask God for healing. Pray for the protection of your health.

❧

Chapter 9 - The Decision to Leave

God Sightings

- Now that I understood I was married to a narcissist, I was more keenly aware of Ben's behavior and our interactions.
- God gave me the strength and desire to protect my sons from Ben, regardless of the consequences I would face.
- God allowed me to experience the suffering I did for me to realize I had no choice but to leave Ben.

SCRIPTURES

Psalm 9:9 The Lord is a stronghold for the oppressed, a stronghold in times of trouble.

Nahum 1:7 The Lord is good, a stronghold in the day of trouble, and He knows those who take refuge in Him.

2 Timothy 2:15 Do your best to present yourself to God as one approved, a worker who has no need to be ashamed, rightly handling the word of truth.

JOURNAL PROMPTS

- If you have made the decision to leave your toxic relationship, how have you planned your departure?
- Many victims of narcissistic abuse have had the unfortunate experience of their husband's narcissistic rage. Thinking back upon an episode of rage, what brought it on? How did you deal with it? How do you feel even now as you think back?

STARTERS FOR YOUR PRAYERS

When you anticipate another episode of narcissistic rage, pray for God to protect you. May He speak truth to you when your husband falsely accuses you.

~

Chapter 10 - My Independence Day

God Sightings

- Danielle's yearlong home renovations were completed just in time for her to offer us a safe place to stay after we left.
- God gave me the courage to follow through and tell Ben that we were leaving.
- I was thankful that God blessed us with freedom.

Scriptures

John 8:36 So if the Son sets you free, you will be free indeed.

Galatians 5:1 For freedom Christ has set us free; stand firm therefore, and do not submit again to a yoke of slavery.

Psalm 118:5 Out of my distress I called on the Lord; the Lord answered me and set me free.

Journal Prompts

- What would freedom look like to you? What are you most looking forward to once you are free?
- If you are unable to create a physical safe space for yourself, in what ways are you able to seek shelter from the storm through your faith?

STARTERS FOR YOUR PRAYERS

We may not always understand it now, but God's timing is always perfect. Ask God for patience when you are in a period of waiting.

~

Chapter 11 - Love Bombs Away

GOD SIGHTINGS

- My good friend, Anna, warned me about typical narcissist behavior and prepared me for what might happen. She was right about the "love bombing" that followed after we left Ben. There are critical terms and phrases associated with narcissistic abuse and it's beneficial for victims and survivors to be aware of them. Please see the glossary in the back of this book for more information.
- God placed Bethany in my path that day in Target for a reason.
- I began to realize that I was not alone in this journey.

SCRIPTURES

Proverbs 16:16 How much better to get wisdom than gold! To get understanding is to be chosen rather than silver.

Proverbs 19:20-21 Listen to advice and accept instruction, that you may gain wisdom in the future. Many are the plans in the mind of a man, but it is the purpose of the Lord that will stand.

Proverbs 27:17 Iron sharpens iron, and one man sharpens another.

JOURNAL PROMPTS

- Knowledge is power. Are you familiar with all the terms associated with narcissistic abuse? Research and learn terms that are new to you.
- Do you find yourself challenged by loneliness? If so, what can you to do feel less lonely?

STARTERS FOR YOUR PRAYERS

There is much to learn about narcissistic abuse. Pray for God to give you wisdom and knowledge as you seek understanding.

∼

Chapter 12 - Abrupt Regression

GOD SIGHTINGS

- I sincerely hoped that Ben would be able to make the necessary changes, and I was encouraged to see him making such efforts.

- Knowing Ben's track record and wanting to protect our peace, I committed to not returning home immediately.
- Ben's absence at the VBS performance was an indication that he was no longer serious about taking responsibility for his past actions.

SCRIPTURES

2 Corinthians 5:17 Therefore, if anyone is in Christ, he is a new creation. The old has passed away; behold, the new has come.

1 Corinthians 16:14 Let all that you do be done in love.

Hebrews 4:12 For the word of God is living and active, sharper than any two-edged sword, piercing to the division of soul and of spirit, of joints and of marrow, and discerning the thoughts and intentions of the heart.

JOURNAL PROMPTS

- Narcissistic abuse is cyclical and goes from the creation of tension to an episode of abuse followed by remorse, and an eventual honeymoon period. The madness then starts all over again. How have you seen this in your marriage?
- It takes an average of seven times for a woman to leave an abusive relationship (McAdams, 2017). What steps can you take to strengthen your resolve?

Starters for Your Prayers

The healing journey can often be confusing. Pray for discernment as you deal with the narcissist and his ways.

Chapter 13 - Four Walls Don't Make a Home

God Sightings

- Despite our chaotic family circumstances, the boys were happy and enjoyed their summer.
- God orchestrated the ideal apartment for us with specific details, availability, and timing.
- The boys' assurance that they were comfortable in our new accommodations because they felt safe in our new home.

Scriptures

Psalm 127:3-5 Behold, children are a heritage from the LORD, the fruit of the womb a reward. Like arrows in the hand of a warrior are the children of one's youth. Blessed is the man who fills his quiver with them! He shall not be put to shame when he speaks with his enemies in the gate.

Psalm 66:5 Come and see what God has done: he is awesome in his deeds toward the children of man.

Isaiah 4:6 There will be a booth for shade by day from the heat, and for a refuge and a shelter from the storm and rain.

JOURNAL PROMPTS

- Whether you are still in your toxic environment or planning to leave, how can you create a safe space for yourself?
- If you have kids, how have they been affected by narcissistic abuse?

STARTERS FOR YOUR PRAYERS

Children are deeply affected by the narcissist's hurtful words. Pray for them to hear God's voice louder than that of their narcissistic father.

Chapter 14 - But, God, I Don't Want to Meet with a Lawyer

GOD SIGHTINGS

- Megan opted not to take my case for legal separation and recommended that I try to work on my marriage for the time being.
- Ben and I met with our church family to sort through the difficulties in our marriage.
- I learned that I had cPTSD and needed to get help to address the triggers.

SCRIPTURES

Psalm 37:5 Commit your way to the Lord; trust in him, and he will act.

Proverbs 11:14 Where there is no guidance, a people falls, but in an abundance of counselors there is safety.

Jeremiah 30:17 For I will restore health to you, and your wounds I will heal, declares the Lord...

JOURNAL PROMPTS

- If you are suffering from PTSD, what are some of your triggers? What are you doing to handle them better?
- When I spoke to my therapist about PTSD, she recommended eye movement desensitization and reprocessing (EMDR) to get rid of my triggers. Have you considered this kind of therapy to get past your triggers?

STARTERS FOR YOUR PRAYERS

Post-traumatic stress disorder can be terribly debilitating. If you find yourself suffering from this, ask God to help you resolve your triggers.

∾

Chapter 15 - God Sightings

GOD SIGHTINGS

- I cried out to God and asked Him to direct my steps as I felt so lost navigating through my marriage.
- God used Serena, Julie, and Sabine to answer my prayer request for encouragement. From my interactions, I gathered that God wanted me to keep fighting for my marriage.
- Doves made their first appearance, and they became a regular and symbolic representation of God's presence for me and the boys.

SCRIPTURES

Psalm 34:17-18 When the righteous cry for help, the Lord hears and delivers them out of all their troubles. The Lord is near to the brokenhearted and saves the crushed in spirit.

Proverbs 27:9 Oil and perfume make the heart glad, and the sweetness of a friend comes from his earnest counsel.

Psalm 55:4-8 My heart is in anguish within me; the terrors of death have fallen upon me. Fear and trembling come upon me, and horror overwhelms me. And I say, "Oh, that I had wings like a dove! I would fly away and be at rest; yes, I would wander far away; I would lodge in the wilderness; I would hurry to find a shelter from the raging wind and tempest."

Proverbs 13:20 Whoever walks with the wise becomes wise, but the companion of fools will suffer harm.

JOURNAL PROMPTS

- Looking at your journey, who are some people you feel God has placed in your life to help you? How have you been encouraged by them? What have they taught you?
- What can you identify as God sightings in your story?

STARTERS FOR YOUR PRAYERS

It is easy to be overwhelmed as you fight this battle. Know that you are not alone. The battle is the Lord's. Thank God for fighting this battle with you and for you.

Chapter 16 - God Sends More Messengers

GOD SIGHTINGS

- As I spent more time praying for wisdom and discernment in my situation, God strengthened me.
- I prayed for a job and shared very specific job requirements and God delivered!
- Danielle's Bible study friend, Cindy, has the gift of prophecy and prayed over me and my situation.

SCRIPTURES

Isaiah 41:10 Fear not, for I am with you; do not be dismayed, for I am your God; I will strengthen you, I will help you, I will uphold you with my righteous right hand.

Romans 12:12 Rejoice in hope, be patient in tribulation, be constant in prayer.

2 Peter 1:21 For no prophecy was ever produced by the will of man, but men spoke from God as they were carried along by the Holy Spirit.

Romans 12:6 Having gifts that differ according to the grace given to us, let us use them: if prophecy, in proportion to our faith...

JOURNAL PROMPTS

- How has God strengthened you in your journey? In what ways would you want God to give you more strength or courage?
- What have you learned in your interactions from others? Make notes of the wisdom you receive as you will learn to reflect on these words in difficult moments.

STARTERS FOR YOUR PRAYERS

God hears your prayers, so be bold and pray specifically. Cry out to Him. What is your most pressing need right now?

Bring it to the Father. He already knows what you are going through.

~

Chapter 17 - God Rescues Me

GOD SIGHTINGS

- Though disappointed by Ben's absence, Ryan demonstrated strength at his promotion ceremony.
- Ben had divorce papers served to me just mere hours after I signed legal separation papers. God's timing is always perfect, and, in this case, He gave me far more than I had thought to ask.
- I recognize that God rescued me from my marriage and looked forward to a new life of freedom.

SCRIPTURES

Psalm 68:5 Father of the fatherless and protector of widows is God in his holy habitation.

Psalm 31:15 My times are in your hand; rescue me from the hand of my enemies and from my persecutors!

Isaiah 43:1-2 But now thus says the Lord, he who created you, O Jacob, he who formed you, O Israel: "Fear not, for I have redeemed you; I have called you by name, you are mine. When you pass through the waters, I will be with you; and through the rivers, they shall not over-whelm you; when you walk through fire you shall not be burned, and the flame shall not consume you.

Psalm 37:7 Be still before the Lord and wait patiently for him; fret not yourself over the one who prospers in his way, over the man who carries out evil devices!

JOURNAL PROMPTS

- Are you stuck in your marriage because you continually hear that "God hates divorce?" God also hates abuse. How might this change the way you think about your marriage?
- The MEND Project, Patrick Weaver Ministries, and Leslie Vernick are solid resources for victims and survivors. What resources are equipping you as you learn more about narcissistic abuse? Do you feel conflicted about your faith and what actions you might be forced to take with your marriage?

STARTERS FOR YOUR PRAYERS

We have a loving Father who cares for us. He understands the frustrations of this trial. If you feel conflicted, pray that God will find ways to show you His love and give you peace as you make difficult decisions.

～

Chapter 18 - God Provides

GOD SIGHTINGS

- I was relieved to learn that our financial needs would be met in the short term.
- I was blessed by the positive work environment of my new job and the wonderful colleagues I had.
- With the dove flying across my windshield, God showed me His presence yet again.

SCRIPTURES

2 Corinthians 9:8 And God is able to make all grace abound to you, so that having all sufficiency in all things at all times, you may abound in every good work.

1 Thessalonians 5:11 Therefore encourage one another and build one another up, just as you are doing.

Joshua 1:5 No man shall be able to stand before you all the days of your life. Just as I was with Moses, so I will be with you. I will not leave you or forsake you.

JOURNAL PROMPTS

- What are some ways God has provided for you and your family? Are you confident that He will meet all your needs?
- How has God's perfect timing played a role in your life?

STARTERS FOR YOUR PRAYERS

Thank God for His presence in your life. Ask Him to walk closely by your side as you go through your suffering.

~

Chapter 19 - Did God Just Answer My Prayer?

GOD SIGHTINGS

- With the change of attorneys, I was thankful that I had trustworthy legal experts on my team.
- I was hopeful that Ben had finally concluded that he was ill and was earnest in receiving help.
- I was able to rest and practice self-care when the boys were with Ben on his custody weekends.

SCRIPTURES

Proverbs 2:9-11 Then you will understand righteousness and justice and equity, every good path; for wisdom will come into your heart, and knowledge will be pleasant to your soul; discretion will watch over you, understanding will guard you...

Psalm 31:18 Let the lying lips be mute, which speak insolently against the righteous in pride and contempt.

Matthew 11:28-30 Come to me, all who labor and are heavy laden, and I will give you rest. Take my yoke upon you, and learn from me, for I am gentle and lowly in heart, and you will find rest for your souls. For my yoke is easy, and my burden is light.

JOURNAL PROMPTS

- Hoovering is a term used to describe what a narcissist might do to suck you back into interacting with him. Have you experienced hoovering yourself? If so, how did you handle it?
- If you have kids with the narcissist in your life, have you experienced parental alienation? What are some ways that you can strengthen the relationship you have with your children?

STARTERS FOR YOUR PRAYERS

If you are contemplating divorce, invest the time to seek out the best legal representation you can afford. Pray for God to lead you to the right attorney; someone who will understand your needs, has had previous experience in divorces involving narcissists, and will fiercely protect you and your children.

~

Chapter 20 - Scripture Comes Alive

GOD SIGHTINGS

- As you draw closer to God, He will draw closer to you. God showed me relevant Scripture in my difficult circumstances.

- I loved sharing God's Word with the boys as we went through BSF together. It was vital that the boys had a firm foundation of faith.
- Ryan experienced Ben's gaslighting firsthand confirming that Ben cannot be trusted in telling the truth.

SCRIPTURES

Romans 12:19 Beloved, never avenge yourselves, but leave it to the wrath of God, for it is written, "Vengeance is mine, I will repay, says the Lord."

Daniel 3:24-25 Then King Nebuchadnezzar was astonished and rose up in haste. He declared to his counselors, "Did we not cast three men bound into the fire?" They answered and said to the king, "True, O king." He answered and said, "But I see four men unbound, walking in the midst of the fire, and they are not hurt; and the appearance of the fourth is like a son of the gods."

2 Chronicles 20:15 And he said, "Listen, all Judah and inhabitants of Jerusalem and King Jehoshaphat: Thus says the Lord to you, 'Do not be afraid and do not be dismayed at this great horde, for the battle is not yours but God's.'

Proverbs 3:4-5 So you will find favor and good success in the sight of God and man. Trust in the Lord with all your heart, and do not lean on your own understanding.

JOURNAL PROMPTS

- Have you found, like I did, that old familiar Bible verses began to come to life in your trial? Which Bible verses have been brought you hope, encouragement, strength, or peace?
- How has your husband gaslighted you or your children?

STARTERS FOR YOUR PRAYERS

Looking at where you are now in your marriage, in what areas might you need support? Pray and ask God to lead you to Scripture that will encourage you.

Chapter 21 - God Exposes Ben's Lies

GOD SIGHTINGS

- God's Word was a source of strength for me during mediation.
- God answered my prayer that I would be protected. Judge Hughes recognized that Ben was a bully and did what he could to make me feel safe.
- Judge Hughes saw through Ben's lies and mediation details ruled in my favor.

SCRIPTURES

Mark 11:24 Therefore I tell you, whatever you ask in prayer, believe that you have received it, and it will be yours.

Deuteronomy 31:6 Be strong and courageous. Do not fear or be in dread of them, for it is the Lord your God who goes with you. He will not leave you or forsake you.

Matthew 7:7 Ask, and it will be given to you; seek, and you will find; knock, and it will be opened to you.

Luke 12:2-3 Nothing is covered up that will not be revealed, or hidden that will not be known. Therefore whatever you have said in the dark shall be heard in the light, and what you have whispered in private rooms shall be proclaimed on the housetops.

JOURNAL PROMPTS

- How can God protect you in your current circumstances?
- Do you feel closer to or further from God as you work through this difficult time?

STARTERS FOR YOUR PRAYERS

When you feel intimidated by the narcissist, remember that you have the same God that gave David the courage to slay a giant. Pray confidently that God will protect you in legal proceedings and that the truth will be revealed.

Chapter 22 - "Be Patient"

GOD SIGHTINGS

- The boys and I moved into a more permanent environment when we purchased a townhome.
- I fasted in the hopes that I would hear God's voice more clearly and received God's message to "be patient."
- I learned to trust God's timing as I tried to figure out what He meant by "be patient."

SCRIPTURES

John 10:27 My sheep hear my voice, and I know them, and they follow me.

Exodus 14:14 The Lord will fight for you, and you have only to be silent.

Psalm 27:14 Wait for the Lord; be strong, and let your heart take courage; wait for the Lord!

Psalm 94:19 When the cares of my heart are many, your consolations cheer my soul.

JOURNAL PROMPTS

- Have you fasted to hear God's voice? If so, what did you learn from your fast? If you haven't fasted before, is this something you might consider?

- In what ways is God speaking to you?

STARTERS FOR YOUR PRAYERS

Fasting is powerful. If you decide to fast, pray for God to reveal His will for you. Pray for a breakthrough in your circumstances.

~

Chapter 23 - More Clarity

GOD SIGHTINGS

- God reminded me that multiple times along my journey His timing had always been perfect, and I was led to continue trusting Him in my current circumstances.
- I received a vision of Danielle and me at the morgue to identify Ben's body and wondered if it might be something sent from God.
- I realized that God may be telling me that Ben will soon leave us and if that truly was the case, I promised to be honorable to him.

SCRIPTURES

Isaiah 33:6 And he will be the stability of your times, abundance of salvation, wisdom, and knowledge; the fear of the Lord is Zion's treasure.

Matthew 6:34 Therefore do not be anxious about tomorrow, for tomorrow will be anxious for itself. Sufficient for the day is its own trouble.

Exodus 22:23 If you do mistreat them, and they cry out to me, I will surely hear their cry...

JOURNAL PROMPTS

- Do you find yourself unable to sleep because you are worried? What do you ruminate about?
- If you consider the past, what might have you done differently? What helped you the most?

STARTERS FOR YOUR PRAYERS

Do not allow yourself to be overwhelmed. Get proper rest. If you find yourself staying up at night with racing thoughts, pray for God to give you peace and to quiet your mind.

~

Chapter 24 - Unexpected Events

GOD SIGHTINGS

- I'm thankful for God's protection that the boys didn't go to Ben's as scheduled.
- Ben realized he needed help and checked into a mental health facility.

- After all that Ben had put us through, neither Ryan nor I felt obligated to visit Ben at the hospital.

SCRIPTURES

Psalm 91:2 I will say to the Lord, "My refuge and my fortress, my God, in whom I trust."

Psalm 27:1 The Lord is my light and my salvation; whom shall I fear? The Lord is the stronghold of my life; of whom shall I be afraid?

Psalm 31:3-4 For you are my rock and my fortress; and for your name's sake you lead me and guide me; you take me out of the net they have hidden for me, for you are my refuge.

JOURNAL PROMPTS

- In what ways have you felt God's protection?
- Do you ever fear for your own safety or that of your children? What are steps you can take to ensure your safety?

STARTERS FOR YOUR PRAYERS

Even in the worst of times, there are things for which we can be grateful. Sit quietly with God and think about where you are in your battle. What can you be thankful for despite this difficult season? Thank God for these silver linings.

~

Chapter 25 - I'm Numb

GOD SIGHTINGS

- Still in shock from the news of Ben's sudden passing, I notified Danielle who assured me that I had her full support in whatever I needed.
- God gave me positive memories of Ben as I tried to fall asleep.
- Greg helped me understand that Ben can no longer hurt us.

SCRIPTURES

Proverbs 17:17 A friend loves at all times, and a brother is born for adversity.

Matthew 5:4 Blessed are those who mourn, for they shall be comforted.

John 5:24 Truly, truly, I say to you, whoever hears my word and believes him who sent me has eternal life. He does not come into judgment, but has passed from death to life.

John 16:22 So also you have sorrow now, but I will see you again, and your hearts will rejoice, and no one will take your joy from you.

JOURNAL PROMPTS

- In what practical ways can your support team help you?
- If you find it difficult to ask for help, why do you think that is?

STARTERS FOR YOUR PRAYERS

Don't feel as if you must shoulder the weight alone. Seek help from others. Often, people want to help, but just don't know how. If you find it difficult to ask for help, pray that God will equip you with boldness.

⁓

Chapter 26 - Surrounded by Love

GOD SIGHTINGS

- In the days after Ben's passing, I never felt alone as friends and family rushed to support us.
- Our community sustained us and met our every need.
- God helped me to forgive Ben and I was able to plan his memorial as I know he would have wanted.

SCRIPTURES

2 Timothy 2:7 Think over what I say, for the Lord will give you understanding in everything.

Galatians 6:2 Bear one another's burdens, and so fulfill the law of Christ.

2 Corinthians 1:3-4 Blessed be the God and Father of our Lord Jesus Christ, the Father of mercies and God of all comfort, who comforts us in all our affliction, so that we may be able to comfort those who are in any affliction, with the comfort with which we ourselves are comforted by God.

Psalm 119:71 It is good for me that I was afflicted, that I might learn your statutes.

JOURNAL PROMPTS

- Forgiveness can help bring healing. Are you at a place where you are able to forgive the abuser in your life? If not, what would it take for you to forgive?
- In what areas of your life can you praise God for His comfort?

STARTERS FOR YOUR PRAYERS

If you struggle to forgive the narcissist, pray for the Spirit to soften your heart. Forgiveness is not something to benefit the receiver, but rather for you to shed the weight and create distance from the pain.

~

Chapter 27 - God's Presence

GOD SIGHTINGS

- Unsure of how to eulogize Ben, I was guided by the Holy Spirit.
- Once again, God used a dove in our story. As the dove circled overhead three times, it was as if Ben was saying a final good-bye to each of the boys.
- With the hectic prior weeks coming to a close with Ben's memorial, I felt a sense of peace and woke up with an excitement for the future.

SCRIPTURES

Job 10:12 You have granted me life and steadfast love, and your care has preserved my spirit.

1 Peter 5:10 And after you have suffered a little while, the God of all grace, who has called you to his eternal glory in Christ, will himself restore, confirm, strengthen, and establish you.

2 Thessalonians 3:16 Now may the Lord of peace himself give you peace at all times in every way. The Lord be with you all.

JOURNAL PROMPTS

- When's the last time you felt God's presence?
- What makes you feel peaceful? How are you able to bring more peace into your life?

Starters for Your Prayers

When it's non-stop chaos as you deal with the narcissist in your life, you need to carve out time to rest under our Creator's wings. If you feel like everything is spiraling out of control, pray for God to take you in, protect you, and give you space to breathe.

~

Chapter 28 - God Confirms His Rescue

God Sightings

- I felt a sense of relief when God released me from all guilt after learning of the affair.
- I'm thankful that the timing of the revelation came after Ben's memorial.
- God saw everything that I didn't. I'm reminded of Corrie Ten Boom's story of the embroidery crown. On one side, we see a tangled mess of colorful thread, but on the other side is a beautifully stitched crown. When I was going through all the chaos with Ben, all I saw was the tangled mess. God, however, saw a perfect crown. We must trust God in our circumstances because "God knows what we do not know" (Everydaywiththeking, 2022).

SCRIPTURES

Proverbs 12:26 One who is righteous is a guide to his neighbor, but the way of the wicked leads them astray.

James 1:12 Blessed is the man who remains steadfast under trial, for when he has stood the test he will receive the crown of life, which God has promised to those who love him.

Jeremiah 29:11 For I know the plans I have for you, declares the Lord, plans for welfare and not for evil, to give you a future and a hope.

Romans 8:28 And we know that for those who love God all things work together for good, for those who are called according to his purpose.

JOURNAL PROMPTS

- Despite your difficult circumstances, what can you be thankful for?
- God is faithful. Recall moments where God has provided for you in the past. Are you confident that He can and will provide for you again?

STARTERS FOR YOUR PRAYERS

Though we might not understand everything as it's happening, we can rest in the knowledge that God is faithful. Take a moment to recall His faithfulness and ask that He meets you again, according to His will.

NARCISSISTIC ABUSE
GLOSSARY

~

BREAD CRUMBING

The act of luring someone on without the intention of becoming romantically involved with them.

COGNITIVE DISSONANCE

The confusion experienced when two or more concepts contradict one another.

DEVALUATION (DISCARD)

A part of the narcissistic abuse cycle when the narcissist finds their victim no longer useful.

FLYING MONKEYS

A term taken from the movie *The Wizard of Oz* to refer to those who help the narcissist manipulate and dominate others.

GASLIGHTING

The psychological manipulation of a person, frequently over time, that causes the victim to doubt the validity of their own ideas, perceptions of reality, or recollections.

GOLDEN CHILD

The narcissist parent's favorite child who can do no wrong (the opposite of the scapegoat).

GREY ROCK METHOD

The strategy of being emotionally unresponsive, dull, and behaving like a rock so that the narcissist isn't given any attention.

HOOVERING

The manipulative behavior of a narcissist who tries to lure you back after you have ended the relationship.

HYPERVIGILANCE

Often a symptom of PTSD where a sufferer is constantly on high alert.

LOVE BOMB

An emotional manipulation in which the narcissist lavishes the victim with excessive affection, flattery, and presents to get their attention and praise.

NARCISSISTIC PERSONALITY DISORDER (NPD)

A personality disorder in which the sufferer has an overinflated feeling of their own importance, a strong desire for excessive attention and praise, strained relationships, and a lack of empathy for others.

NARCISSISTIC RAGE

The inclination of narcissists to explode into an all-out rage at their victims.

NARCISSISTIC SUPPLY

The psychological need for narcissists to demand a steady source of attention and praise.

NO CONTACT

The boundary set by survivors where they block or have no ongoing interactions with narcissists.

PARENTAL ALIENATION

The psychological manipulation of a child that results in rejection of the other parent.

PROJECTION

The transferring of a characteristic or trait onto another person.

POST-TRAUMATIC STRESS DISORDER (PTSD)

A condition that arises when a victim experiences situations that induce extreme terror, dread, or despair.

SCAPEGOAT

The child of the narcissist parent that receives blame for the actions of the narcissist (the opposite of the golden child).

SMEAR CAMPAIGN

When the narcissist spreads misinformation to cause you conflict and turns loved ones against you.

TRAUMA BOND

An unhealthy attachment disorder that occurs between the narcissist and the victim.

SPECIAL REQUEST

Would You Like to Help Another Survivor?
Pay it Forward

If you are a survivor of narcissistic abuse, you likely suffered in silence for many years. I hope that by reading *Can't You Smell the Smoke?* you have gained some insight and feel validated and not as alone as when you first started reading.

If you have found this book valuable, would you consider taking a brief moment to leave an honest review? Your review just might give another survivor the courage to face their own challenges.

Thank you.

SEEKING EXTRA SUPPORT?

If you would like additional support
as you deal with the narcissist in your life,
we'd love to have you join our
private Facebook group:
Christian Support for Narcissistic Abuse Recovery

Don't forget to grab your free guide!

Your 7 Step Journey to Narcissistic Abuse Recovery
www.TrilliumSage.com

ALSO BY SYDNEY KOH

Dealing with the Unavoidable Narcissist in Your Life
A STRATEGIC BLUEPRINT FOR COPING WITH
DIFFICULT RELATIONSHIPS

"...informative, compassionate, and insightful read."
"...reminds me I am not alone and there is help..."
"...will help you find your inner strength."

ACKNOWLEDGMENTS

∼

So much heartfelt appreciation...

God...for Your faithfulness, goodness, protection, and provision. This is Your story. Thank You for allowing me to play a small part in it.

Mom and Dad...for establishing a foundation of faith in our family. Your constant support of me and the boys will never be forgotten.

MK...for your wisdom and for somehow making me smile on my darkest days. You'll forever be my favorite sister.

ML...for always being my protective little brother. You mean the world to me. You're the best funcle the boys could ever have.

RS...for being a wise old soul and protecting your little bros through the pain. I am in awe of your resilience. Love you, you stinker.

GS...for allowing God to use you to encourage me. I will be forever grateful for your important role in my story and how you care for me. Love you, G.

IS...for keeping me on my toes. You have taken on so many

challenges in life and beaten them down one by one. I'm ever so proud of you. I love you, kiddo.

DG...for *everything*. Just not enough words. I know being on call 24/7 is a tall order. You are the best PR rep I could never afford.

AR...for loving on me and standing by me through *all* of life's trials. I'm glad you let a nerd sit behind you in Rosen's class.

JG...for always being a ready ear and for fiercely protecting me.

CL...for enthusiastically inviting me to do Bible study with you, for praying unceasingly, and for sharing my love of French pastries.

Our framily–F/D/N/B...for welcoming me and the monkeys into your home and for adopting me on those weekends the boys were with their father. Casibling love always.

HR...for modeling what the Father's unconditional love looks like and for loving my boys as your own.

My HCC small group...for the countless prayers, endless discussions, and tireless encouragement.

JP...for spurring me on in my faith and for your constant prayers over my boys.

OL...for making me laugh in even the most painful moments. Thank you for praying over me.

JM...for the regular check-ins and assurance that God's got me in His hands.

BG...for always pointing my journey back to God. You've got a beautiful soul.

Dr. AB...for helping my boys unpack their pain and for helping me understand them.

Pastor CL...for your many prayers and guidance. Thank you.

HN...for being a friend to MS.

AY...for your care and expertise. You have no idea how much peace the gift of redecorating our home provided us.

PL...for yummy moments and sharing your wisdom.

JC and DM...for your guidance in the faith.

SF...for your sage advice, constant encouragement, and always keeping God at the center.

J...for your role in my story. I hope to one day cross paths with you again.

SP...for your transparency and giving me hope. Your faith is inspirational.

SR...for your ever willing ear and texting me prayers when I needed them most.

JR...for being our family's prayer warrior. I appreciate you always looking out for me and my guys.

LB...for giving me hope for my future. You are one of the strongest women I've ever met.

JS...for being a bright light through the darkness.

JC...for bringing so much positivity and comfort.

TH...for coffee meet-ups and helping me understand my circumstances.

RC...for always being so real and giving me strength to step out in boldness.

JA...for making sure I made myself a priority when my world was falling apart.

CH...for your guidance on mental health issues and for praying over my family.

MY and LF...for sharing just the right words at just the right time.

DM, FG, YL...for all the work you put into helping with the apartment.

LF...for sitting with me when being alone in the quiet was too much.

HCC family...for surrounding my family with love on our darkest days.

My Life Group...for always praying over me and encouraging me in my writing.

LH...for revealing to me that I was married to a narcissist.

MC and AC...for being the best legal team I could pray for.

JM...for being my SIC who constantly shares wisdom and God's truths with me.

NB and TG...for wisely leading our group and giving me the time and space to write.

KN and DS...for keeping me focused. How did I find you two among the 12k? But God!

NC...for your talent and wordsmithing abilities.

SE/AuthorizeMe...for convincing me that my story is not meant to be kept to myself.

CH/Winged Publications...for giving me the opportunity to share my story and help the silent community of hurting victims.

Yogi...for unconditionally loving the boys and me. You are the (perfect) dog RS asked for that fateful night. Love you, Mr. YoYo.

ABOUT THE AUTHOR

Sydney Koh was born in Singapore and raised in sunny Southern California. After receiving her degree in Chemistry from the University of California, Irvine, Sydney immersed herself into the world of biotechnology both in the United States and Asia. Once she became a mom, she devoted all her time and energy to her three boys. Her life with them consists of traveling, camping, snowboarding, cooking, and eating. During precious downtime, Sydney enjoys naps, beaches, wine, and her 100-pound German Shepherd mix, Yogi. Sydney's personal life is the basis for her inspirational memoir *Can't You Smell the Smoke?* Having escaped her marriage of 15 years to a narcissist husband, she now seeks to empower others in their quest to regain their sense of self – transforming victims into survivors. Her deepest hope in sharing her poignant life story is to walk alongside those experiencing unthinkable heartbreak and anguish and to give them hope that divine deliverance is possible.

REFERENCES

~

Anchored Abode. (n.d.). *Scapegoat Definition: The Narcissist Family In Depth*.anchoredabode.com. Retrieved September 17, 2022, from https://anchoredabode.com/2019/09/03/scapegoat-definition-narcissism/.

Bhandari, S. (2005, March 25). *SSRI Antidepressants for Bipolar Disorder*. WebMD. Retrieved July 2, 2022, from https://www.webmd.com/bipolar-disorder/bipolar-ssris.

Brazier, Y. (2020, September 30). *All about narcissistic personality disorder*. www.medicalnewstoday.com. https://www.medicalnewstoday.com/articles/9741#diagnosis.

ChoosingTherapy.com. (2022, August 24). *What Is Narcissistic Supply?* Choosing Therapy. Retrieved September 17, 2022, from https://www.choosingtherapy.com/narcissistic-supply/.

Cirino, E. (2018, October 3). *Understanding Situational Depression*. Healthline. Retrieved June 23, 2022, from https://www.healthline.com/health/depression/situational-depression.

Corelli, C. (2022, September 17). *Narcissist Hoovering: How to Deal With It*. Carla Corelli. Retrieved September 17, 2022, from https://www.carlacorelli.com/narcissistic-abuse-recovery/narcissist-hoovering-how-to-deal-with-it/.

Crawford, K. (2022, August 1). *What Is a Trauma Bond?* Narcissist Abuse Support. Retrieved September 17, 2022, from https://narcissistabusesupport.com/what-is-a-trauma-bond/.

Dellwo, A. (2021, November 23). *What Are the Differences: Bipolar vs. Narcissistic Personality Disorder?* Verywell Health. Retrieved July 2, 2022, from https://www.verywellhealth.com/bipolar-disorder-vs-narcissistic-personality-disorder-5210087.

Everydaywiththeking, V. A. P. B. (2022, August 23). *Embroidery Lesson – Corrie ten Boom*. Every Day With the King. Retrieved September 15, 2022, from https://everydaywiththeking.com/2021/11/04/embroidery-lesson-corrie-ten-boom/.

Gotter, A. (2018, August 23). *What Is Hypervigilance?* Healthline. Retrieved

September 17, 2022, from https://www.healthline.com/health/hypervigi
lance.

Luv, T. (2021, September 16). *What Is Post-Narcissist Stress Disorder (PNSD) and its 3 Major Symptoms*. The Minds Journal. Retrieved September 17, 2022, from https://themindsjournal.com/post-narcissist-stress-pnsd/.

McAdams, L. (2017, March 15). *Why does it take seven times to leave an abusive relationship? - Safe Space Workplace*. Safe Space Workplace - DFV Training & Coaching Provider. Retrieved September 15, 2022, from https://safespaceworkplace.com/2017/03/15/take-seven-times-leave-abusive-relationship.

Narcissistic personality disorder - Symptoms and causes. (2017, November 18). Mayo Clinic. Retrieved September 17, 2022, from https://www.mayoclinic.org/diseases-conditions/narcissistic-personality-disorder/symptoms-causes/syc-20366662.

Pace, R. (2021, December 7). *What Is Breadcrumbing: 10 Signs & How to Deal With It*. Marriage Advice - Expert Marriage Tips & Advice. Retrieved September 17, 2022, from https://www.marriage.com/advice/relationship/what-is-breadcrumbing/.

Protassius. (2022, August 18). *Grey rock*. The Book of Narcissism. Retrieved September 17, 2022, from https://bookofnarcissism.com/knowledge-base/grey_rock/.

Psychology Today. (2009, March 17). *https://www.psychologytoday.com/us/basics/cognitive-dissonance*. www.psychologytoday.com. Retrieved September 17, 2022, from https://www.psychologytoday.com/us/ba-sics/cognitive-dissonance.

Raypole, C. (2021, April 6). *Narcissistic Personality Disorder: Traits and Symptoms*. Psych Central. Retrieved June 23, 2022, from https://psych central.com/disorders/narcissistic-personality-disorder/symptoms#narcis sism-diagnosis.

Sagman, D., MD, & Tohen, M., MD. (2020, November 16). *Comorbidity in Bipolar Disorder*. Psychiatric Times. Retrieved July 2, 2022, from https://www.psychiatrictimes.com/view/comorbidity-bipolar-disorder.

Shaman, T. L. (2022, August 15). *Narcissists & Psychopaths: Surviving the Smear Campaign*. YouMeMindBody. Retrieved September 17, 2022, from https://youmemindbody.com/mental-health/Narcissists-Psychopaths-Surviving-The-Smear-Campaign.

Stines, B. P. S. (2018, January 15). *Coping with Narcissistic Parental Alien-ation? Consider These Tips*. GoodTherapy.org Therapy Blog. Retrieved September 17, 2022, from https://www.goodtherapy.org/blog/coping-with-narcissistic-parental-alienation-consider-these-tips.

Telloian, C. (2021, November 10). *The Tactic Narcissistic Personalities Often Use on Empathic People*. Psych Central. Retrieved September 17, 2022, from https://psychcentral.com/disorders/narcissistic-projection.

Ways to Tell If Someone Is Gaslighting You. (2022, July 25). Verywell Mind. Retrieved September 17, 2022, from https://www.verywellmind.com/is-someone-gaslighting-you-4147470.

Weil, A. (2017, December 13). *Phantosmia: Smelling Smoke All The Time?* https://www.drweil.com. Retrieved June 23, 2022, from https://www.drweil.com/health-wellness/body-mind-spirit/disease-disorders/phantosmia-smelling-smoke-all-the-time/.

What Is a Flying Monkey | Narcissist Smear Campaign At Work | Mindset Therapy. (n.d.). Retrieved September 17, 2022, from https://www.mindsettherapyonline.com/blog/what-is-a-flying-monkey-narcissist-smear-campaign-at-work.

What Is Narcissistic Rage? (2021, November 13). Verywell Mind. Retrieved September 17, 2022, from https://www.verywellmind.com/what-is-narcissistic-rage-5183744.

Why Do Narcissists Discard You? | Mindset Therapy. (n.d.). Retrieved September 17, 2022, from https://www.mindsettherapyonline.com/blog/why-do-narcissists-discard-you.

CPSIA information can be obtained
at www.ICGtesting.com
Printed in the USA
BVHW051243060223
657963BV00014B/1070